FREE YOUR MIND, LISTEN WITH YOUR HEART

Healing the Journey from Courage to Love

Maya Linkinoska

Free your Mind, Listen with your Heart
Copyright © 2021 Maya Linkinoska
First published in 2021

Print: 978-1-76124-010-2
E-book: 978-1-76124-011-9
Hardback: 978-1-76124-009-6

All rights reserved. No part of this book may be reproduced, stored in a retrieval system, or transmitted by any means (electronic, mechanical, photocopying, recording, or otherwise) without written permission from the author.

Because of the dynamic nature of the Internet, any web addresses or links contained in this book may have changed since publication and may no longer be valid. The information in this book is based on the author's experiences and opinions. The views expressed in this book are solely those of the author and do not necessarily reflect the views of the publisher; the publisher hereby disclaims any responsibility for them.

The author of this book does not dispense any form of medical, legal, financial, or technical advice either directly or indirectly. The intent of the author is solely to provide information of a general nature to help you in your quest for personal development and growth. In the event you use any of the information in this book, the author and the publisher assume no responsibility for your actions. If any form of expert assistance is required, the services of a competent professional should be sought.

Publishing information
Publishing, design, and production facilitated by Passionpreneur Publishing,
A division of Passionpreneur Organization Pty Ltd, ABN: 48640637529

www.PassionpreneurPublishing.com
Melbourne, VIC | Australia

A personal transformational journey of self-discovery, walking and healing the path from courage to love and learning to trust intuition and divine guidance.

Dedication: *To all the living beings, especially the animals, students and teachers, who have crossed or shared my path on my life journey, guiding me and supporting me to find and fulfill my life mission and purpose.*

Purpose: *To leave a legacy for truth and freedom seekers, to be the voice of the silence, the voice for animals and nature, to help unite humanity with the core and essence of our being.*

CONTENTS

Introduction	1
From Happiness to Joy	11
Chapter 1: 2020 — New Decade, New Beginnings	15
Chapter 2: The Power of Intuition	21
Chapter 3: The Power of Silence	27
Chapter 4: Realignment and Balance	31
Chapter 5: Raising Consciousness	47
Chapter 6: Healing with Movement and Sound	55
Chapter 7: Practice Gratitude	63
Chapter 8: The Practice of Letting Go	67
Chapter 9: Animal Connection	71

Chapter 10: Silent Language	79
Chapter 11: Life between Lives or "LBL"	89
Chapter 12: Shamanic Journey	97
Chapter 13: Finding My Inner Artist	101
Chapter 14: 2020 Awakening of Humanity	105
Chapter 15: Ancestral Healing	111
Chapter 16: My Personal Guide to Freedom	115
Chapter 17: New Moon, New Cycle, New Earth	123
Chapter 18: Spiritual Laws and Practices	131
Chapter 19: The Path to Freedom	135
Chapter 20: Finding Connection in Paradise	141

"A man who can unlock his soul is set free."

— GREEK PHILOSOPHER IAMBLICHUS

INTRODUCTION

Have you ever wondered where you come from? Do you ever ask yourself questions like: Do I have a soul? What is a soul? Is a soul infinite? How old is my soul? Does it have a shape, a color? From where did the soul originate? Who is the creator? Where do we go after we die? I do — all these questions and more.

As a child, from around the age of six, I often wondered where the end of the world was. My father, my mother, my older sister, and I traveled a lot by car, touring the Balkan countries of Europe, going to different places for summer and winter holidays or long weekends. I loved looking out the window as my father drove for many hours, day and night, observing and absorbing everything I could. I was searching for the place where the world ended. I imagined that one day we would reach a dead-end street with a wooden sign proclaiming: *End of the World.* In my mind's eye, the road ended at a broken hill or mountain where I saw white smoke rising from a hole in the ground. It marked a separation into the unknown.

I was always interested in where life and after-life met. I pursued answers with a curious child-like mind, entering a self-discovery and exploration journey of the soul.

In my first book, *Unveiling the Path to Happiness,* I shared my journey to self-discovery and finding inner peace and happiness. This was my exploration of the questions: *Where is my soul? How can I connect to it on a deeper level? What happens to my soul when I die? How can I be happy and fulfilled all the time on a deep level?*

This book aims to delve further into my life purpose and my soul gifts, my having had the courage and willingness to go deep within to find the source of human existence. My research has centered on the questions of *what is a soul?* and *how are we all connected?* — not only humans but animals and all other living beings. *What is that thing that joins us together that we call "oneness"?*

Until the age of 28, I was highly focused on academia and my corporate career. I always loved school and

INTRODUCTION

learning. This was evident from my early childhood days as I accompanied my sister, four years older than me, to her school classes, well before it was my time to start school. I started working in the corporate world at the age of 18 and became a manager at 22 with my first company relocation from Auckland, New Zealand, to Sydney, Australia, in 2005 when I was only 23 years old. I completed my master's degree in maritime law in London in 2008, and until 2012 I lived a safe and structured life: a life within the lines.

In 2012 at the age of 29, in the midst of my Saturn return cycle,[1] I had a spiritual awakening in which I reconnected to my inner child and my creative soul. I followed a spiritual path that led me back from London to Australia (on a one-way ticket, without any plans or much money) where I spent my life from 30 to 38. For the first two years, I traveled around Australia with one suitcase and very little money. I wanted to put all my life skills to the test and see where life would take me if I had no job, no security, and no money — only me and my inner guide, my inner compass. This is how I challenged myself beyond means I knew were possible

---

1 An astrological quarter-life crisis. Some call it the make it or break it time in your life. It happens when the planet Saturn comes back to meet your natal Saturn; it takes 29.5 years to return to where it was when you were born.

and discovered parts of me I did not know existed and found gifts I never knew I had.

In this book, I want to share my discovery of the gifts that bring us joy, happiness, purpose, meaning, and abundance. Our work should flow with ease and not be difficult. Our efforts and output when we use our gifts should be easy and flowing. We should be attracting abundance in return for creating with love and joy. I want to show you how it's possible to bridge the gap between our personal purpose, which is usually centered on our job, security, and personal goals, to our divine or higher purpose, which is the mission of our soul, why we came here, what gifts we have, what lessons we need to learn, and what mission or tasks we have for this lifetime.

As I finish writing this book, I am 39 years old and living in Dubai, United Arab Emirates. I am back working in the corporate world as a regional legal manager in the maritime industry; in my free time, I write, dance, create art, practice my spirituality, and give back to humanity, animals, and our environment. I aim for balance and harmony between work and my personal life — for a balance between our personal and divine purpose.

INTRODUCTION

"Do not wait for leaders; do it alone, person to person."[2]

— Mother Teresa

My life journey is inspired by Mother Teresa, who was born in my city Skopje, Macedonia, not far from the neighborhood where I was born. Mother Teresa, now known as Saint Teresa of Calcutta, shared many life lessons throughout her time on Earth, most of which centered on love, compassion, helping others, and maintaining humility. She embodied a wonderful example for all of us to follow — to simply love and give help to others without asking for anything in return.[3]

"Live simply so others may simply live."

— Mother Teresa[4]

In my first book, *Unveiling the Path to Happiness*, I share my journey to finding inner peace and happiness, which

---

[2] https://www.powerofpositivity.com/10-life-lessons-we-can-learn-from-mother-teresa/
[3] https://www.powerofpositivity.com/10-life-lessons-we-can-learn-from-mother-teresa/
[4] https://www.biography.com/religious-figure/mother-teresa

started with exploring and improving the relationship with self and others. I shared some stories from my life experiences about healing my body of stored trauma, connecting to my higher self through yoga, dance, and meditation, and finding more about my soul and my gifts via *akasha*[5] and the Akashic Records.[6]

Many people operate from their headspace, where they cannot hear what their body and soul, Mother Nature, and the animals are communicating. This connection does not happen overnight; it requires practice, and I keep working on it every day. I share in this book the journey I have taken to shift from my headspace to my heart space and connect to the sounds of nature, to the spirit; I hear the messages of my soul through intuition, feeling, and guidance from the Universe.

When I was a child, as soon as I finished school, I would rush home to the garden to say hello to our rabbits and play with them. I always enjoyed spending time with animals, especially our parrots and our rabbits. I also

---

5   Sanskrit word for space or ether in which a record of past events is imprinted.
6   A compendium of all universal events, thoughts, words, emotions, and intent ever to have occurred in the past, present or future in terms of all entities and life forms, not just humans. Wikipedia.

INTRODUCTION

loved my grandparents' goats and baby goats. It became clear to me that there was some form of communication and connection between me and animals. We all know that animals cannot speak a language the way humans can. So, there's no point in expecting this from an animal. But humans have a choice. Humans can choose to speak, or they can be silent. Rabbits are quiet and silent animals, but this doesn't mean they don't feel or think. So, if I also choose a silent language and enter this shared zone, I can learn a lot from animals through my heart and intuition. I can feel what they feel; I can see what they see. They can either send visual images to communicate or they can send feelings, vibes, and smells and communicate through body language.

Everything has a vibration, a sound, a symbol or picture, and messages are constantly transmitting between us. It's like tuning into a radio station — messages flow between humans, between animals, and between humans and animals.

We all share an invisible language we are born with — telepathy and universal consciousness. This book will remind you of the many gifts we are all born with, gifts that you can use throughout your life to make your life more vibrant and joyful.

In his essay "A Defence of Poetry" (1821),[7] the English poet Percy Bysshe Shelley wrote: 'Poets are the unacknowledged legislators of the world.'

Words hold so much power. Each word has its own vibration and frequency. I started writing poetry and short stories when I was only six years old, so I always knew this was one of my gifts. Music, poetry, dance, storytelling, and films are the spiritual glue that binds us together as human beings. It is the connection between our body and our soul. Creativity and self-expression are essential for human connection and development. One of my gifts is to communicate the unspoken, and the mediums I choose are the written word, dance, and art.

Intuition, especially claircognizance (the inner knowing) has always been my strength, and I have known this from a very young age. Since learning how to read at the age of five, I have always loved books and knowledge. Growing up, I had a library of books in my bedroom, and my favorite present was always to receive a book, especially a signed book by the author with a personalized message for me.

When I was going to primary school, I would choose a book before bedtime, touch the book, open the book,

---

[7] https://en.wikipedia.org/wiki/A_Defence_of_Poetry

INTRODUCTION

turn a few pages, close the book, place it under my pillow, and go to sleep. In the morning, when I woke up, I felt like I had read the book in my sleep. I had all this knowledge, and when I did exams at school, I almost always got 100 percent; I was a top student in all my subjects.

Through this, what I learned is that knowledge and wisdom are within me. I am not learning through reading a book; instead, I get reminded of what I already know, awakening my inner genie. When writing my books, I share my personal life experience about something. Then I find the words to match, or existing principles or theories to express what I experienced or felt, rather than learning about something by reading and then finding the experience to match.

FROM HAPPINESS TO JOY

What is the difference between happiness and joy?

When I experienced strong emotions of happiness, I realized they were temporary feelings. I found that the feelings might last a day or two; they were not long-lasting or permanent.

I started searching for something deeper within while on my trip to India in February of 2020. I wanted a feeling or emotion that was long-lasting and to which I could easily connect. I decided to explore joy.

What is joy?

While sitting by the Ganges River in Rishikesh, the holy city of India, overlooking the Himalayan mountains, I set my intentions for the next chapter of my life and a new decade. In the Chinese zodiac, 2020 was the year of the Rat, and the element metal, which signifies new beginnings and turns misfortune into good fortune.

> *"Rats are clever, quick thinkers; successful, but content with living a quiet and peaceful life."*[8]

This seems congruent with what we are currently experiencing with the COVID-19 pandemic situation; it is about reconnecting to ourselves on a deeper level and learning to be content with living a quiet, simple, and peaceful life. I can most certainly agree that the situation has brought good fortune to me because it was during the lockdown that I completed and published my first book.

While at home in lockdown in Melbourne, I also completed an online course called "Awaken the Five Elements with Belly Dancing and Ceremony." I learned all about the five elements and our personalities based on which element or elements we are. Metal is about rising and spirituality, so 2020 being the year of the metal rat made sense.

---

8   https://chinesenewyear.net/zodiac/rat/

For me, 2020, was all about finding the true meaning of joy and experiencing different levels of joy within my body. I uncovered five things that brought me joy:

1. Spending time in nature
2. Spending time with animals
3. Dancing
4. Painting
5. Singing

These are the things that bring me peace:

1. Spending time alone, in bushland or the beach, listening to the sounds of nature
2. Yin Yoga and meditation
3. Being in the company of animals
4. Dancing, music, and instruments (sound healing)
5. Being in the now and living in a flow

Now I will briefly explore freedom. What does freedom mean to me?

It means:

1. Feeling safe and comfortable in my own body.

2. Trusting my intuition and living from a place of flow and ease, knowing there is a unique divine plan for me.
3. Doing the things I love and enjoy, as mentioned above.
4. Knowing that I am an infinite being, a soul residing inside and outside a specific body for a single lifetime.
5. Knowing that I have free will and choices in life, a knowledge that comes from obtaining a higher level of consciousness.

"Integrity gives you real freedom because you have nothing to fear since you have nothing to hide."

— Zig Ziglar

1

2020 — NEW DECADE, NEW BEGINNINGS

> "The purpose of life is to discover your gift. The work of life is to develop it. The meaning of life is to give your gift away."
>
> — DAVID VISCOTT[9]

The year 2020 started with a bang!

Earlier, my cousin Katerina had come to visit me in Melbourne from Macedonia. We traveled to Sydney for two days because she told me it was her wish to be in Sydney for New Year, and I wanted to contribute to making her wish come true. We booked a boat trip, which

---

9   https://quoteinvestigator.com/2014/06/16/purpose-gift/#note-9172-2

included a buffet dinner and dancing, to watch the fireworks on Sydney Harbor. It was a spectacular night. The fireworks on the Sydney Harbor Bridge were magnificent, and I was blown away by being so close to this magic. To me, stars and fireworks are all about magic.

One month later, in February, I left my corporate job as a Group Risk and Claims Manager in Melbourne and travelled to Rishikesh, India, for a seven-day yoga retreat. India was a transformational journey for me. Dipping in the famous Ganges River and going in the caves in the Himalayan mountains to see the cavemen or "baba" was mind-blowing. Literally, mind-blowing — I felt my crown chakra crack open when I arrived in India!

I spent seven days in Rishikesh, which sits at the foot of the Himalayan mountains. It is a city famous for yoga and gods and goddesses. At the crown of the Himalayas on Mount Tibet is where the vortex of the crown chakra lies. I can say that I felt a physical and spiritual awakening and transformation on another level during this trip. I participated in a beautiful fire ceremony with an Indian Guru by the Ganges and enjoyed delicious vegetarian food.

By the time I arrived back in Melbourne, the world was in the throes of a global pandemic known as COVID-19,

2020 — NEW DECADE, NEW BEGINNINGS

and we had to be in isolation for about three months. All borders were closed, people were not allowed to travel, and we could only leave our houses under strict criteria.

I was still going through powerful integration and transformation, having just returned from India, so I saw this isolation as an opportunity to spend time with myself and focus on personal development. It is during this time that I wrote my first book *Unveiling the Path to Happiness*. I also started painting more regularly, developed daily and weekly rituals, and completed my soul-realignment course, where I learned how to connect to and read the Akashic Records. I spent more time with my rabbits and my parrot Gucci and worked on my animal communication and connection skills.

It was a peaceful and productive three months for me, especially on a spiritual and personal development level. I feel so much gratitude and appreciation for having had that time to go inwards and focus deeper on myself and my spiritual journey. Having seen the poverty in India just before the pandemic, I had greater awareness and appreciation about life and different ways of life. I was touched and transformed to see how many people in India live on the streets and live a simple and basic life. It was not very difficult for me to give up on unnecessary luxuries during the pandemic. These souls living in India have divinely chosen to experience that kind of life. In life, we have light and dark for a reason. You cannot know what light is without seeing the dark — like the yin and yang. And by choosing that life, you can establish a deep spiritual connection to yourself and your spirituality: a life not driven by ego but by love, empathy, and compassion.

I also enjoyed learning about the Indian gods and goddesses and their stories. Living with faith and connection to a higher purpose or God is what keeps humanity moving and evolving. We are all on a unique soul path or journey. By tapping into self-discovery, deep in our divine spiritual being, our soul-purpose and divine soul gifts are what re-connects us to our Source and reminds us we are here to experience a life journey we chose to create for ourselves. Let's not forget the power we have within us to design our own life experiences and tackle our life challenges and lessons with awareness, consciousness, and confidence as empowered spiritual beings. It is not an easy path to take to live a conscious life, but it is a path well worth pursuing once you learn how to master life skills.

Having completed a soul-realignment course and the Akashic Records, I have an increased awareness of where my soul originates, what my spiritual path is about, and the lessons I am seeking from my spiritual experience as a human on Earth. We are usually here to teach what we are here to learn. Our biggest fears and challenges are often the keys to unlocking the door of our lessons. One example is I cannot ride a bicycle. I tried many times as a child and could not do it. I can balance well in yoga and body-balance classes with my eyes closed, but I cannot ride a bicycle. My lesson is, therefore, to master balance.

I am here to be a bridge between animals, humans, nature — in general, all living beings. My last name, Linkinoska, contains the word "link" and "linkin," and my first name, Maya, means love, magic, and the Goddess of Spring and Rebirth, so I find the clues about my purpose just by looking at my name. Names are said to have vibrational power to bring us to our dharma or path of destiny.

I often talk about my association with seeing the numbers 11:11. Let me explain what it is.

The number 11:11 is an awakening code and represents easy access to the higher realms of the spirit. Our soul exists in light and codes. When you consciously see 11:11, it brings a message and frequency from the spirit, signifying that there is an open doorway to you through which you can access higher divine guidance, expanded consciousness, and incredible frequency, love, and healing.

It carries guidance and frequency from the spirit. It is a call to tune into the direct angelic guidance and the higher levels of light and codes of awakening available to you right here and now.[10]

When you see numbers like 11:11, 12:12, 1:11, 2:22, 3:33, 4:44, and so on, these are open gateways to connect to your spirit guides, angels, or higher self for inner guidance and messages. Stop what you are doing, take a deep breath, and go into meditation to access your messages or codes. You can read in detail what each number means on the link in the footnotes.

> *"Coincidence is God's way of remaining anonymous."*
>
> — Albert Einstein

---

10   https://www.ask-angels.com/spiritual-guidance/1111-what-does-it-mean/

2

THE POWER OF INTUITION

> "The intuitive mind is a sacred gift, and the rational mind is a faithful servant. We have created a society that honours the servant and has forgotten the gift."
>
> — ALBERT EINSTEIN

Our intuition serves as the path of our connection to the Divine or God. I have been practicing my intuitive gifts with card readings for the last ten years and have found this method has served me well, providing me with good guidance and helping me learn to trust my intuition.

After learning about the Akashic Records or the Book of Our Soul, I bought some new cards to start using as additional guidance with my readings. I bought *The*

FREE YOUR MIND, LISTEN WITH YOUR HEART

Starseed Oracle by Rebecca Campbell and Danielle Noel. It's a beautiful baby blue and pink set, which resonated with me when I was guided to buy it. I usually trust my own guidance and intuition, and I am very quick at making decisions and acting when I find something that resonates with me.

I remember the night when I chose to get my very first Akashic reading. I was lying in bed feeling restless. I couldn't sleep and was guided to go on my mobile phone, from where I was guided to search on "Akashic Records." When I found my first reader, Michelle, the time was 11:11 pm; and when I decided to purchase and pay for her reading, the time was 12:12 am. I knew I was on the right path and went to sleep peacefully after that.

Tonight, I opened my new Starseed oracle cards and did a reading for myself.

The first card I picked was Messenger. Sirius star energy, bringing harmony and balance. This card says I am part of a lineage of souls that have dedicated their lives to the upliftment of the planet. I am here to re-plant the sacredness of life, bringing harmony between the masculine and feminine and bringing greater balance to the world, to Planet Earth.

The next card I picked was "We the Hathors. Deep love. Mother's milk. Birth as a portal." This card is about allowing Mother Nature to hold me and nurture me. To rest more deeply in the Mother's arms and to trust my journey. I am being called to raise the sacred feminine energy, the energy of creation and birth. To nurture myself and others. To surrender, to be held, and to hold. To expand and share the love.

The last card I picked was Stars Ancestors. It reminded me to unlock the hidden power of my ancestors and inner wisdom, especially in connection to the stars. The message is calling me to tap into the part of me that remembers and knows — to unlock my soul's memories and use my creativity to find creative solutions. "Creativity happens when we put together two things that don't belong."

I enjoyed the reading I did for myself this evening; it strongly resonated with me and gave me some guidance and a reminder of what I am here to do.

When I read cards or need to connect to my intuition for guidance and messages, I often play soft, gentle music. I find it easier to connect to my spirit and intuition when I listen to music.

FREE YOUR MIND, LISTEN WITH YOUR HEART

I also purchased a set of the Akashic Tarot oracle cards and did my first reading tonight. The first card I picked, Two Worlds, was 100 percent accurate for me. It is a conflict between the physical or external world and the spiritual or inner world. I find it hard to maintain a balance and live in both worlds at the same time. The card said that in a past life I had chosen only a spiritual path, and in another life, only the physical or material path, and that I had struggled to find deeper meaning in one or the other alone. The message was to bring my spiritual self to every situation in my personal life.

The second card was one of my favorites: The Archangel Michael. It reminds me of the greater power within me, the strength and courage needed to act and to call on his energy to uplift me when required, so I can thrive and keep going forward to complete my goals and missions.

The last card was Five of Forces. It is about taking action to create what I want in my life. I feel the time has now come for me to take the necessary action to bring forward to the world my divine gifts and my sacred creations that I have been producing in my cocoon over the last three months of isolation.

Using oracle cards is a fun and easy way to get guidance via your intuition and spirit guides. It's a great way for beginners to start their spiritual journey, which is how I started mine about twelve years ago when I realized that picking certain cards and meeting certain people was not just a coincidence. I shared more about this in my first book.

3

THE POWER OF SILENCE

"We need to find God, and he cannot be found in noise and restlessness. God is the friend of silence. See how nature — trees, flowers, grass — grows in silence; see the stars, the moon and the sun, how they move in silence … We need silence to be able to touch souls."[11]

— MOTHER TERESA

I discovered the power of silence in 2013 when I went on my first ten-day Vipassana silence retreat in the Blue

---

[11] https://www.goodreads.com/quotes/220034-we-need-to-find-god-and-he-cannot-be-found

Mountains just outside Sydney. This experience opened my mind and heart to all the possibilities within me, without the need to think or speak. It is where I found my true inner voice that sparked my creativity and got me doing more art and dancing.

Vipassanā or vipaśyanā — literally, "without-seeing," "without, seeing" — means to see things as they really are. It is a Buddhist term that is often translated as "insight." Vipassana is one of India's most ancient meditation techniques and was taught in India more than 2500 years ago as a universal remedy for universal ills — that is, it is an art of living.

The technique of Vipassana meditation is taught at the ten-day residential course during which participants learn the basics of the method and practice it to experience its benefits. There are no charges for the course. All expenses are met by donations from people who, having completed the course and experienced the benefits, wish to allow others to also benefit. So, it's like a pay-it-forward-type donation.

Vipassana is said to be:

- a technique that will eradicate suffering
- a method of mental purification that allows one to face life's tensions and problems in a calm, balanced way
- an art of living that one can use to make positive contributions to society.[12]

Vipassana meditation aims at the highest spiritual goals of total liberation and full enlightenment. Its purpose is not to cure physical disease, although as a by-product of mental purification, many psychosomatic diseases are eradicated. In fact, Vipassana eliminates the three causes of all unhappiness: craving, aversion, and ignorance. With continued practice, the meditation releases the tensions developed in everyday life, untying the knots tied by the old habit of reacting in an unbalanced way to pleasant and unpleasant situations.[13]

In my first book, I shared my experience from a silent retreat I did in the mountains in Italy, one of the most rewarding experiences of my life. When we can master

---

12 https://www.dhamma.org/en/portal/student_apps/10163849/pages/3/edit
13 https://www.dhamma.org/en/portal/student_apps/10163849/pages/3/edit

FREE YOUR MIND, LISTEN WITH YOUR HEART

the silence, there is so much magic that happens. We can connect to nature, to ether, hear the trees, the animals, the stars, the moon, the planets, our spirit guides, and more. We can smell the roses and feel the beauty of life.

4

REALIGNMENT AND BALANCE

Chakras, Auras, and Soul

They say riding a bicycle is easy. "It's just like riding a bike," they say when referring to anything easy.

I cannot ride a bike. So, I practice balance in other ways. As a child, I loved gymnastics. Now I do yoga, body balance classes, aligning and balancing my chakras, to name a few. My challenge, therefore, is to bring this balance to other things. I am good at finding balance within myself, but when it comes to using objects like a bicycle, or when in relationships with other people, I often lose my balance. So, this is what I need to work on in my life. Once I master this, I can teach others who have this same problem.

Color also has vibration and different frequencies that are often used for healing in art, light, or color therapy. I once experienced a light therapy session in the Hale Clinic in London. During this session, I had a magical and vivid experience of my soul, seeing the colors of the chakras with my eyes closed. Chakras are like a wheel of energy or a vortex at different locations and colors. They are found in the human body, in animals, on Planet Earth, and on other planets too.

According to Michael Newton's research into the soul, chakras are a spiritual expression of individuality through physical manifestations.[14]

During the COVID-19 lockdown in Melbourne, I took the opportunity to complete an online course called Chakra Dance To Change Your Life. I first came across chakra dance about five years ago when I bought the book *Chakradance* by Natalie Southgate. With it came a bonus of fourteen audio downloads, and I started dancing the chakras to this music. The online course was great. It came with seven modules, one for each chakra, and videos of Natalie sharing practical information about each chakra, some dance movements, how to dance each chakra, and music corresponding to the

---

14   *Destiny of Souls*, Michael Newton.

vibration of each chakra, followed by a meditation for each chakra.

I will share some information here about my experience on the seven-day ritual with the chakra dance.

Day 1: Root or base chakra (Muladhara)
We started the day with a brief explanation of the root chakra. The color of this chakra is red. It is all about stability, grounding, safety, security.

Red is my favorite color. My parents always dressed me in red as a baby, so I grew up surrounded by the color red.

I am also a fire sign and have a lot of the fire element in me. Sometimes I have experienced too much fire or excess in my root chakra and so I have a lot of this energy. It is important to use this energy creatively and resourcefully.

I have felt strong and balanced in my root chakra for the last five years. The times when I have not felt grounded are when I am dancing a lot on my toes and wearing high-heeled shoes, so my feet are not flat on the floor, and when I travel and spend a lot of time up in the air.

About five years ago, I stopped wearing high-heeled shoes and started consciously to practice grounding by either walking barefoot in nature or by doing yoga, or the chakra dance for root chakra. This restored my root chakra balance, making it strong.

When this chakra is unbalanced or lacking, it shows up in the person as fear, instability, insecurity, attachments to material things, or addictions.

On Planet Earth, the base chakra is said to be located in Mount Shasta in California.

Day 2: Sacral chakra (Svadhisthana)
The color of this chakra is orange. It lies in our lower abdomen under our belly button and is all about our emotions, joy, creativity, pleasure, and sexuality.

If this chakra is unbalanced, you experience the negative emotions of shame and guilt, also being shy, having sexual issues, allergies, and eating disorders. Negative emotions or trauma stored in this chakra can cause blockages and various problems in our energy flow and how we express ourselves.

Belly dancing and yin yoga are two of my favorite healing modalities to practice for shifting unresolved energy in the sacral chakra.

On Planet Earth, the sacral chakra is said to be located in Lake Titicaca in South America, on the borders of Peru and Bolivia.

Day 3: Solar Plexus chakra (Manipura)

This chakra lies in our higher abdomen, above the belly button. It is about personal power and manifestation and relates to self-esteem, warrior energy, and transformation.[15]

Currently, this is where I have some blocks that I want to release.

When I arrived in Australia in 2012, I was greatly triggered and activated in my solar plexus chakra about my identity and self-worth.

During my travels and spiritual studies around Australia from 2012 to 2015, I discovered that Uluru/Ayers Rock in the middle of Australia is where the solar plexus energy vortex of the planet lies. Many people worldwide are attracted to Australia on their self-discovery journey because it activates their solar plexus chakra and invites them to look deeper within themselves and their identity. For many years during the Gold Rushes in Australia, many

---

15   https://www.bemytravelmuse.com/healing-earth-chakras/

people immigrated to Australia for this precious metal, but many didn't find the gold they expected. Instead, they found the gold within themselves. They were invited to look deeper within themselves and question their identity, their beliefs, self-worth, and purpose in life.

Before that, many early settlers were brought to Australia as convicts and the country was used as an open jail. These people were stripped of their values, their identity, and their families. Yet they were called to look deeper within to find their true being and who they really were, apart from the role of father, or brother, or uncle, or friend.

I take this opportunity to honor Australia and the Uluru/Ayers Rock formation for the wisdom and power that it holds. It is an enlightened formation, holding the energy of enlightenment.[16] It cracks open our hearts to find our true gifts and powers within. When I moved to Australia in 2012, buying a one-way ticket from London and going into the unknown with two suitcases of clothes and shoes, I knew it wasn't going to be an easy journey. The painful lessons I have learned on this golden path

---

[16] According to a vibration reading done using scalar waves technology by Elena Bensonoff and Alejando Ferradas.

in Australia, in reconnecting with my divine being and my true self, have been very rewarding indeed, much like finding gold.

Today, I wear a yellow dress, and I dance the solar plexus chakra guided by Natalie and the music. Strengthening my identity is the message I receive. I have been on a personal transformation and experimental journey for the last fifteen years, and now it's time to ground my new identity — the improved, stronger, and wiser version of me.

Yellow is the color of the solar plexus chakra. On the morning of the dance, I drank pineapple juice. I had an omelet for breakfast and pumpkin soup for lunch. I ate yellow; I dressed in yellow; I bought yellow flowers and painted in yellow. Surrounding myself in yellow activated the solar plexus chakra and prepared it for work. I released negative belief patterns and any negative emotions held about my personal power and identity. It was also the day when the full moon was rising so that made the release even more potent. During the dance, I found myself connecting with my power animal and my animal spirit guides. I released suppressed anger and frustration through the dance and prepared my body for meditation and relaxation.

Day 4: Heart chakra (*Anahata*)

After the solar plexus dance, I felt I needed to fill the space I created in my body with some love. I did a receiving meditation to open my heart chakra before I started with the dance.

My life lesson of light-heartedness falls here. I often have the challenge of being too serious and being too hard on myself, placing high expectations on myself, taking on too many responsibilities, and setting high standards for myself and others. In the past, when things didn't go how I had planned or envisioned them, I became sad and disappointed, so these feelings set in the heart chakra, making it feel heavy and blocked.

Loss, grief, heartbreak also fall in this chakra space, which can make our heart chakra unbalanced.

During the last six months, I had to find new homes for 18 of my rabbits and my parrots. This was not easy for me. The process of loss and grief takes time. I cried a lot, and the emotions of loss and grief set in my heart chakra. I write more about my animals in another chapter.

As I hold onto emotional loss and grief in my heart, every time I dance the heart chakra and do the meditation, I release new layers of what don't serve me, letting go of loss and grief and sadness, and forgive myself and others for times I have held these emotions in my heart. Practicing not to take things personally is an ongoing lesson and journey.

I painted a green painting I call Dancing Goddess, so when I dance the heart chakra, I dance in front of this painting and wear a green dress.

On Planet Earth, the heart chakra is said to be located in Glastonbury (Stonehenge) and Shaftesbury in England.

Day 5: Throat chakra (Vishuddaha)
This chakra is blue and is located on our throat, both front and back. One way to open this chakra is to spend time by the sea or ocean. Another way is by singing and speaking the truth.

This chakra, for me, was restricted. When I was a little girl, I wanted to sing, but when I started singing, I remember my sister telling me to stop, and then when I went to singing classes, my teacher told me I could not sing well. So, I accepted this might not be my gift and stopped trying to evolve my voice. During my 30s, I started using my voice more, and unresolved issues emerged related to my voice and my lack of confidence about singing. An Akashic Records reading told me I was given a secondary god spark, which is an extra gift, around the age of 28, and this resonated with me. I spoke and stood up for myself and what I wanted, I left London and my job, I moved from a back-office job to being on the front by being in direct sales, and I started life coaching and public speaking.

My next goal is to develop my voice further so that I can sing without feeling shame or a lack of confidence. Our voice is also connected to our womb, so the more I sing, the more my womb opens. The throat chakra and sacral chakra are very much connected, shame being stored in the sacral chakra, which then affects my throat chakra and freedom of expression.

On Planet Earth the throat charka lies at three great sites in the Middle East: the Great Pyramid of Giza in Egypt, Mount Sinai in Egypt, and the Mount of Olives in Jerusalem.

Day 6: Third-eye chakra (Ajna)

I love this dance and feel well connected to my intuition, my vision, and third-eye chakra. When I have strong visions, I draw or paint and this helps me with manifestation. I wear indigo-colored clothes and light a candle when I do the third-eye chakra dance. I usually do it in the evening for about 13 minutes, after which I do a five-minute meditation and then go to bed. During my sleep, the clearing process takes place (if there is anything to clear) and then my visions and any messages come in my dreams while I sleep.

On Planet Earth this is a moving chakra — last time it was in Bali.

Day 7: Crown chakra (Sahasrara)

This chakra is on the crown of our head; on Planet Earth, the crown is in the Himalayas in Tibet.

I dress in violet colors and light a violet candle for wisdom. I usually do this dance and meditation at night before going to sleep. After I visited Rishikesh in early 2020, I felt my crown chakra becoming stronger and expanding. I have improved my connection to my Higher Self and God. I am a highly conscious spiritual being living in different dimensions at the same time, creating my own life experiences here on Earth to learn the lessons I came here to learn and share my wisdom and knowledge with others.

I dance the crown chakra regularly to clear any blockages in the path to God or my Higher Self and maintain my healthy connection to the Source.

Mantra for the chakras:
1. Root chakra — I am ...
2. Sacral chakra — I feel ...
3. Solar Plexus chakra — I do ...
4. Heart chakra — I love ...
5. Throat chakra — I speak ...
6. Third-Eye chakra — I see ...
7. Crown chakra — I understand.

Chakras model by Ruth Huber

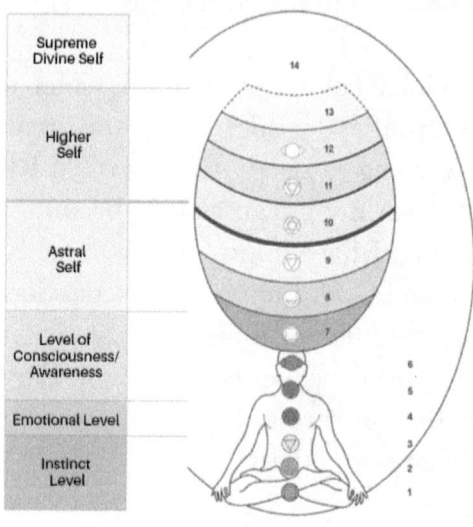

[17]

---

[17] https://www.inspiriert-sein.de/chakra-system-chakren-bedeutung-heilung

REALIGNMENT AND BALANCE

My first chakra realignment with crystals

When I lived in London in 2009, one of the places I lived in was Pan Peninsula in Canary Wharf. I lived on the 34th floor. There was a bar on the top floor, a cinema, a cafe, a restaurant, a swimming pool, a gym, a spa, a sauna, and a wellness center. I lived a life of ease and convenience so I could focus on my full-time job and my studies.

One day I saw a brochure at the wellness center advertising that an energy healer was coming once a week to offer energy healing and alignment with crystals. I was curious to find out what it was all about. It was the first time I had come across this kind of treatment and the first time I'd heard about the chakras. And it was the first time I experienced having the different crystals associated with each of the chakras placed on my body at each chakra location. The energy healer also told me that my energy was not suitable for sauna or high heat, nor a heavy gym workout. I should try something lighter like yoga.

At the time, I had a busy life. My weekdays were spent going to work, having dinner, going to university or studying, and going to the gym, sometimes three times a day. My weekends were spent traveling or studying. I was focused on and dedicated to my career, so I wanted to have good health, which would bring me success in my job and my life.

But after his advice, I changed my routine and gym workouts. I started teaching Zumba part-time after work. I would spend three to four hours each weekend at the nearest Virgin Active gym, doing two Zumba classes, then yoga, then swimming.

People often asked me how I have so much energy and get so much done in a day. One of the secrets is I don't spend my time and energy watching TV. For the entire five years I lived in London, I did not own a TV. My days at home were spent either studying or reading books. On the weekends, I explored life and traveled. If I wanted to watch a movie, I went to the cinema on a Friday night if I wasn't traveling. After I arrived in Australia, for the first three years, again I did not have a TV. I spent most of the time traveling, exploring, relaxing on the beach, or dancing.

If you spend less time watching TV and forming a view about the world from the media, you have more time and energy to spend living your own life and forming your own views about your own reality of life. I apply the same principle to studying, books, and teaching. I do not read a book and then teach theory. I go out with an open mind and heart, live my life, feel my life, have different experiences, and then teach through my own experiences and feelings. I like to develop my own rules, practices, and theories through living and experiencing life.

We are all unique and have our own unique paths in life. We may cross paths with different people, or we may have the same destination, but each path, and how long it takes us to do something or get somewhere, is unique to us. We need to be respectful and understanding of this and live our lives gracefully, without judgment, respecting each other's space, individual needs, boundaries, and purpose. There is no need for humans to compete with each other. The only person we should be competing with is our past self. This is a good measure of how far we have come on our individual journey.

Aura and the soul

Aura is the reflection of the main colors of our chakras, which we manifest in our reality. It can also reflect our gifts and show either an excess or lack of chakra energy. You can look at it like our spiritual body, the unseen expression of our physical manifestation. If you develop and practice your intuition, especially clairvoyance, you can learn how to see auras. Animals also have auras like humans.

Our soul color and color of aura or chakras are not the same.

Here I share some information from Dr. Michael Newton's book *Destiny of Souls*.

> *"The soul is an intelligent light energy. This energy appears to function as vibrational waves similar to electromagnetic force. Like a fingerprint, each soul is unique."*

If you are interested in reading more about soul evolution and life between lives, I highly recommend Dr. Michael Newton's books.

#	LEVEL	COLOR
1	Level I: Beginner	White
2	Level 1: Beginner	Off-white Gray / Grayish with tints of Pink
3	Level II: Lower Intermediate	White and Reddish Pink
4	Level II: Lower Intermediate	Light Orange Yellow with tints of White
5	Level III: Intermediate	Yellow
6	Level III & IV	Deep Gold / Gold with tints of Green
7	Level IV: Upper Intermediate	Green or Brownish Green
8	Level V: Advanced	Light Blue; Light Blue with Gold; Green or Brown tints
9	Level V & VI	Deep Blue
10	Level VI: Highly Advanced	Deep Blue with tints of Purple
11	Higher Levels	Purple

[18]

---

[18] https://mapsforyoufree.blogspot.com/2016/08/david-hawkins-map-of-consciousness.html?m=1

5

RAISING CONSCIOUSNESS

"If you want to find the secrets of the
Universe, think in terms of energy,
frequency and vibration."

— NIKOLA TESLA

Dr. David Hawkins, the author *of Power vs. Force*, created a "Map of Consciousness," which portrays the different energy fields of consciousness and the vibrational levels in which we live.

Our consciousness levels are determined by our emotions, perceptions, attitudes, views, and spiritual beliefs. The map ranges from 1 to 1000, 1 being destruction and

1000 being a fully enlightened being. Hawkins says that the collective level of consciousness is currently at 207, which is the level of courage.

	God-view	Life-view	Level	Scale	Emotion	Process
	Self	Is	Enlightenment	700-1000	Ineffable	Pure Consciousness
	All-Being	Perfect	Peace	600	Bliss	Illumination
	One	Complete	Joy	540	Serenity	Transfiguration
	Loving	Benign	Love	500	Reverence	Revelation
	Wise	Meaningful	Reason	400	Understanding	Abstraction
	Merciful	Harmonious	Acceptance	350	Forgiveness	Transcendence
	Inspiring	Hopeful	Willingness	310	Optimism	Intention
	Enabling	Satisfactory	Neutrality	250	Trust	Release
	Permitting	Feasible	Courage	200	Affirmation	Empowerment
	Indifferent	Demanding	Pride	175	Scorn	Inflation
	Vengeful	Antagonistic	Anger	150	Hate	Aggression
	Denying	Disappointing	Desire	125	Craving	Enslavement
	Punitive	Frightening	Fear	100	Anxiety	Withdrawal
	Disdainful	Tragic	Grief	75	Regret	Despondency
	Condemning	Hopeless	Apathy	50	Despair	Abdication
	Vindictive	Evil	Guilt	30	Blame	Destruction
	Despising	Miserable	Shame	20	Humiliation	Elimination

POWER / FORCE — STRONG / WEAK

[19]

---

19 https://mapsforyoufree.blogspot.com/2016/08/david-hawkins-map-of-consciousness.html?m=1

About a year ago, I came across Elena Bensonoff and Alejandro Ferradas,[20] who perform vibrational frequency readings using a unique system that they developed. They have shared a lot of information regarding the vibrational frequencies of public figures, books, artists, the planets, and sacred places on Earth. I decided to get a reading done for myself and for my parents and some of my pets.

My timeline revealed that I was incarnated at the frequency of 525, which is love. In utero, during my mother's pregnancy with me, I suffered some trauma and dropped to 300 at the time of my birth, which is the level of neutrality. I asked my mother about it; she told me when I was born that I had trouble breathing and turned blue. In my reading, they also told me the emotions that were imprinted on me were the cause of the drop, primarily fear for my life, so this fits in with the story my mother told me.

Later during my childhood, I suffered more trauma, which related to acceptance, discrimination, and judgment, and I dropped to 200, which is the level of courage.

During my adult years, I have been subconsciously on a quest to heal my trauma and increase my vibration back to the love frequency, and above, from the courage

---

20   www.wholistic.com and www.lifeflowcatalyst.com

frequency. This would explain why I went on a healing journey for the last fifteen years and wrote my first book about love and courage. Now my overall vibrational frequency is at 530, which is the level of love. Joy begins at 540, so hopefully, soon I will be vibrating at the level of joy, if not already there.

My creativity was measured at 600, which is peace; my personal development and philanthropy were measured at 500, which is love. In a previous reading, my personal development was measured at 700, which is the level of enlightenment. This is when I was on a break from my professional career and wrote my first book. They say the level of mastery begins at 700, and I shared in my first book that I am here not just to live my life but to master my life. I am on a journey to self-mastery and enlightenment. Indeed, my priority at the time was personal development above all. They also told me that my compassion and empathy levels were 100 percent. I was in the now 95 percent of the time, I was in the joy 94 percent of the time, and my integrity level was 95 percent. Here I want to demonstrate that, if we do the work, it will have a direct impact on our vibrational frequency and therefore the quality of the life we live.

During my reading, I was also told that I was 99 percent aligned with my personal purpose and 95 percent aligned with my divine purpose. In life, we have a personal purpose and a divine purpose. Many people are so focused on their personal purpose that they never get to fulfill their divine purpose. This makes them feel unfulfilled on a deep level without understanding why. They may have a great job or a successful business making lots of money and have lots of friends, but they are only fulfilling their personal purpose and personal goals and haven't done much about their divine purpose or higher purpose, as some call it. Divine purpose is about what we do for humanity from the goodness of our hearts. For example, my personal purpose is to teach, fight for justice, and be a peacemaker. So, my profession is in law and justice, with my main interest in conflict resolution. My divine purpose is to spread love and joy and bring harmony between all living beings.

I have found the work of Dr. Michael Newton very helpful in my research of the soul over the years. To quote Michael Newton, "As a result of the forces of reincarnation we are all products of our past physical lives as well as our spiritual soul experiences between lives."

He says that our soul has imprints from traumas and emotions from our past lives — and so, unknown to our mind, much of our pain, discomfort, and dis-ease is due to unresolved emotional pain and trauma from our past lives. These kinds of things are not obvious to traditional doctors. The systems and technologies that doctors use to find answers are designed for the physical body without considering the soul.

This would explain my journey back in 2012 when I was suffering from shoulder and back pain. I had consulted doctors, physiotherapists, osteopaths, and other types of traditional medicine practitioners without finding the source of my pain, not until I started researching more about the soul and healing trauma, not only from this life but past lives also.

In this book, I want to raise awareness that we should focus on what unites us and not on what separates us. Focus on what we have in common, not on what our differences are. We can incarnate in many different shapes and forms of living beings. We are part of the living Planet Earth, which vibrates at a frequency of 700, making it an enlightened being. Using the above map, we can see we are part of the animal kingdom, with many animals having higher frequencies than most humans. The two animals that I got readings for measured at 500 and 540, respectively, which are the love and joy frequencies. My rabbit Lewis measured at 500, which is love; my rabbit Isabel measured at 540, which is joy, and, interestingly, I always referred to Isabel as a "furry bundle of joy." My parrot Gucci also measured at 540, joy. Most humans, as mentioned, vibrate around the level of 200, which is courage.

If animals and I vibrate at the same frequencies, we are a part of the same soul group. We are all one on a soul level. For this reason, I can connect with animals easily and have heart-to-heart communication with animals.

I share more information about humans and animals later in the book.

When you are in low vibrations, in the alpha contracted state, you may operate from a fight or flight mode and have a limited view of yourself and the world. Being in fight or flight mode drains your vital source of energy, making it difficult to increase your vibration and live a happy and healthy life. What can you do today to transform this way of living? What can you do to stress less and live a life in ease and comfort? The answer is to increase your self-love and do more of what you love and brings you joy. Live from the heart instead of your head where most of the programming is.

When operating at high frequencies, you are seeking oneness and divine connection. Animals are said to have a closer connection to the divine than humans. Animals have an awareness of who they are, why they are here, and where they will go. For humans, our mind can be a limitation, because we forget or lose our connection during birth, usually due to trauma. It is not until we heal the trauma and increase our vibrations that we can feel the oneness and have a strong connection to the Divine.

As we expand and awaken our consciousness, we can handle our emotions better and go through change and transformation, because we are raising our vibration.

How can we raise our vibration? Some tips based on my experience.

- Live in the now. Less fear and less anxiety. More love and joy. Allow things to flow.
- Educate yourself and emphasize personal development
- Stay away from drama and negativity, including the TV and media.
- Practice good deeds by helping others without any expectations.
- Practice appreciation and gratitude daily.
- Listen to positive vibes/music and mantras.
- Spend time in nature and with animals (especially high-vibrational animals like rabbits).

6

HEALING WITH MOVEMENT AND SOUND

"Future medicine will be the medicine of frequencies."

— Albert Einstein

As mentioned earlier, I am highly kinesthetic (intuition type clairsentience, which is about feeling) and so for me, a lot of healing happens through movement, such as dancing, walking, chakra dance, belly dancing, and yoga. Movement shifts the stored emotions or trauma in my body. I use meditation to shift and heal mental images or memories stored in my brain. Holding onto negative memories can prevent us shifting from a place of trauma and moving forward in our lives. Based on my experience, unresolved emotions or trauma within the body can be shifted through a combination of movement and meditation.

Visual people will find meditation beneficial to clearing visual negative memory; kinesthetic people will find dancing, walking, and yoga beneficial; and auditory people will get triggered by sounds or certain words or language. They will find the use of soft loving language and mantras beneficial to replacing the negative sound memory or verbal abuse they may have experienced in their lives.

Once I establish what kind of communication style clients have, I can create a coaching and healing program tailored to their needs. My purpose is not to heal but to guide and facilitate clients to connect with their divine nature and soul purpose. They can then implement rituals and practices in their lives to live a more fulfilled life. It is about the clients reaching their own answers and being guided by their own soul and spirit guides. I am not here to do the work for them but to guide them and support them on their journey as they do the work.

Studying soul realignment and reading the Akashic Records have given me so much clarity about life. I am now able to put all the pieces of the puzzle together. I usually download most of my information and wisdom during the night — in my sleep or during meditation. My intuition and memory become stronger at night, during the week of the full moon, the week of the new moon, when I am in nature, and when I detox or on fasting days.

After completing my soul-realignment course, I did a course called Awaken the 5 Elements through Belly Dance and Ceremony: Ancient Wisdom and Healing Movements to Reclaim Your Power.[21] This course resonated with me. Most of the movements I already did naturally, as I have been a dancer in my past lives in the Middle East and Turkey. I have a strong connection to Middle Eastern music, Arabic, Turkish, and Spanish. What I found interesting in this course was the connection between our personality type and the five elements, which are water, fire, wood, earth, and metal. I have studied the five elements and their connection to our body in my yin yoga course and during my Chinese medicine and acupuncture experiences in London, and so I found it very interesting to learn that the different ways we move our body are connected to which element or elements we are. For example, I am the fire and metal elements, with some water. In the past, I have had fire and wood as my main elements,

---

21 By Dondi Dahlin and Titanya Monique Dahlin

and over the years, I have transformed my wood to metal through my personal development journey. Our personality can change, but our divine nature, our soul gifts, and divine expression remain the same throughout all our lives and incarnations. We just get better and richer at our gifts, or energy centers as we call them in soul realignment, and in each life, we learn to master our gifts and soul expression.

Frequency and sound healing

When I started my awakening and healing process back in 2009, I often used frequency and sound healing therapy. I have always been very connected to music. When I was little, all I wanted to do was sing, and I have enjoyed different kinds of music all my life. I remember when I was a little girl, my father always took me to concerts featuring famous Yugoslavian singers. He would carry me on his shoulders, and I would lift my arms, clapping and singing, trying to catch the attention of the singers. I would also go onto the stage and give them flowers. My father encouraged me in every way possible from a young age to get up on the stage and catch the eye of the public and the media, like going to give flowers to a singer in the middle of a song and then staying on stage and dancing. I often called the local radio station to request songs or for competitions, entering competitions of all kinds, acting and being in school drama, etc.

During my healing journey, I started to listen to different frequency music, which I found mostly on YouTube. I listened to the healing frequency of love, which is 528 Hz,[22] the frequency of 432 Hz to enhance positive energy, the frequency of 852 Hz to activate the pineal gland, and 639 Hz to open the third eye. I also listened to the frequency of God and shamanic healing music, which is 963 Hz and 999 Hz, the frequency associated with our Crown chakra, which is said to reduce tension headaches, stress, and overthinking. I listened to different mantras, like the Goddess Lakshmi and Tibetan healing bell sounds. All of this is available free on YouTube. I would put the music on at night and listen to it while I was falling asleep.

When I was doing my final exams for my master's degree in London, I used to listen to brain activation codes. I cannot remember now where I found these codes because I was intuitively guided to them one night, about twelve years ago. But I do remember waking up and feeling so refreshed that I was able to memorize everything I was learning. I definitely felt a

---

22   According to Dr. Leonard Horowitz.

difference in my brain, especially increased memory levels and alertness.

These are the nine solfeggio frequencies you could listen to for healing:[23]

> 174 Hz — reduces pain physically and energetically
> 285 Hz — leaves your body rejuvenated
> 396 Hz — removes subconscious negative beliefs
> 417 HZ — encourages cells, clears destructive influences
> 528 Hz — repairs DNA, helps transformations
> 639 Hz — balances relationships
> 741 Hz — cleans cells
> 852 Hz — returns spiritual order
> 963 Hz — reconnects you with the spirit

I also did a sound healing course using gongs and Tibetan sound bowls. The most profound thing I learned from this course was the importance of sound and how different sounds have their own frequency and create their own symbol or picture.

During the course, we looked at some videos demonstrating sand on paper and the picture and symbol imprint

---

[23] https://www.youtube.com/watch?v=fPZxIbm1Wbw&t=26476s

that each vibration and frequency left. This reiterates the importance of the words we speak to ourselves and to others. If we speak kind, loving words to ourselves and others, we imprint beautiful cells in our body, and if we speak nasty words to ourselves or others, we imprint negative cells in our body, which may then result in disease.

In the book *The Hidden Messages in Water*, the internationally renowned Japanese scientist Masaru Emoto shows how the influence of our thoughts, words, and feelings on molecules of water can positively impact the earth and our personal health. Using high-speed photography, Dr. Emoto discovered that crystals formed in frozen water reveal changes when specific, concentrated thoughts are directed toward them. He demonstrates the theory by showing how water is deeply connected to our individual and collective consciousness. Drawing from his own research, he describes the ability of water to absorb, hold, and even retransmit human feelings and emotions.

Music, visual images, words written on paper, and photographs also have an impact on the crystal structure. Emoto found that water from clear springs and water that has been exposed to loving words shows brilliant, complex, and colorful snowflake patterns. In contrast, polluted water, or water exposed to negative thoughts, forms incomplete, asymmetrical patterns with dull colors. The implications of this research create a new awareness of how we can positively impact the earth and our personal health.

Emoto believes that since people are 70 percent water, and the Earth is 70 percent water, we can heal our planet and ourselves by consciously expressing love and goodwill.[24]

It is so true when people say we create our own reality, including our own body and the shape we are in. We create this by sound, frequency, vibration, the words we speak, the thoughts we have, and the actions we take. Everything lies within us, and what lies within us is reflected externally in the reality we create for ourselves and our external world.

---

24 https://www.uni-weimar.de/kunst-und-gestaltung/wiki/images/MasaruEmoto.pdf

7

PRACTICE GRATITUDE

I started practicing gratitude regularly in 2014 after purchasing my first Gratitude Diary by Melanie Spears. For each day of the diary, there is a section where you start with what you are grateful for each day. I started to use the diary every day, and this is how my daily gratitude practice began.

Later followed setting intentions, conducting new moon and full moon rituals, and letting go of what no longer served me — mostly by burning things or by writing on a piece of paper what I wanted to let go of and then burning the paper in a small bowl. I also incorporate the practice in my daily morning meditation and sometimes also an evening meditation before I go to bed.

FREE YOUR MIND, LISTEN WITH YOUR HEART

Every morning and night, I include in my meditation practice what I am grateful for each day until I feel the gratitude in my heart, and this helps opening and expanding my heart chakra.

When we live in the now and practice gratitude for what we have and for all that we are in that moment, there are no problems in our life. All our worries and problems dissolve by using this simple yet effective practice.

I do a self-love exercise followed by a dance, I have an altar with various objects and candles, buy fresh flowers and small gifts for myself, make gifts for others, and say prayers. Each morning, I say good morning to myself, my rabbits, my birds, my fish, and my fresh flowers. I also kiss my flowers and my rabbits. I tell them I love them.

I also support artists and creative people. I like to buy things at markets where artists create unique pieces of art, clothing, or house decorations and where I can meet the designer or artist in person.

My gratitude mantra each day is:

> *I appreciate the abundance in my life and allow myself to expand in gratitude, success, and joy every day.*

My gratitude prayer for 2020:

> *Thank you, 2020, for being so kind to me and for all the blessings and lessons you have given me. I could not be the person I am today without the challenges, lessons, and opportunities I have received during 2020.*
>
> *Thank you to my eyes for enabling me to see. Thank you to my ears for enabling me to hear. Thank you to my lips for enabling me to speak. Thank you to my heart for enabling me to love. Thank you to my skin for enabling me to feel. Thank you to my feet for enabling me to connect to Mother Earth. Thank you to all my senses for enabling me to feel, smell, touch, hear. Thank you to my voice for being the song of my soul.*
>
> *Thank you to every soul that has crossed my path and contributed to the greatness of my life. Thank you to Planet Earth, the Cosmos, the Sky, the Sun, the Moon, the Plant Kingdom, and the Animal Kingdom for giving me the most beautiful home for my soul to express itself and live a happy, fulfilled life with love, joy, and peace. Here's to world peace, harmony, and more love!*

8

THE PRACTICE OF LETTING GO

> "People have a hard time letting go
> of their sufferings. Out of fear of the
> unknown, they prefer suffering
> that is familiar."
>
> — THICH NHAT HANH

I remember my very first relationship. I was 16 years old, living in New Zealand. I dated a guy for about eight months. I broke off the relationship by writing a nice letter and placing it in a heart-shaped box with a photo of us in it.

My second relationship lasted nine years. When it ended, I wrote a poem and read the poem aloud when I returned the engagement ring.

Over time, I developed practices for letting go of any unhealthy or negative emotional attachments I had with people.

Now, my practice is not to give the letting-go letter to the person concerned. I write the letter or the poem and then burn it in a fire at the full moon.

As fire can sometimes intensify the energy of what you are putting in it, I would place my items in the fire, which I wanted to transform as well, whether they were thoughts on a piece of paper, or a letter written to someone in which I let them go.

My first lesson in letting go of attachments was when my family relocated from Macedonia to Auckland, New Zealand. I was only 12 years old when we left our home, leaving all our belongings behind except for a suitcase each.

The second time I did this, I moved from Auckland to Sydney. I had to sell my house; however, at that time the company paid for my relocation, and I brought most of my belongings with me in a shipping container.

The third time I moved and experienced some painful lessons of letting go of attachments was when I moved from Sydney to London, on my own, with only two suitcases. Five years later, I once again experienced a painful lesson of letting go when I left London and moved back to New Zealand to stay with my family. Then again, I moved to Australia in 2012. I discuss these moves in more detail in my first book, but what I want to express here is the lesson of letting go of attachments and learning how to access the feelings of safety and freedom within, without being attached to the need to have a physical home and physical things, including money — although I see money more as moving energy than a physical thing.

9

ANIMAL CONNECTION

One of the reasons I decided to write this book was to raise awareness of the importance of animals and the pets we choose in our life — or rather the pets that choose us.

After work each day, I go for a walk. I see many people walking their pets, especially dogs. Some are walked by their owners, but many I see are walked by a dog walker or the nanny or household assistant.

And I notice a disconnect between the animals and the humans. Most of the time, I see people walking their dogs like it is a chore. They are disconnected from the animal, even on their mobile phone, paying no attention to the dog. Little do they know, this very exercise of walking the dog is the most exciting part of the dog's day. The animal is yearning for connection to its owner; it is yearning for some love and attention. This is the time to connect with your pet, enjoy being in the moment with them, learn from them, silence your mind, and enjoy the walk, feeling the connection to the pet. They are not here with us forever; most pets have short life spans. Enjoy the precious moments you have with your pet.

I have learned to appreciate and treasure my pets and every moment I have with them through the pain and suffering I experience every time I lose a pet. Nothing hurts me more than the loss of a beloved pet. It was through this loss and grief experience that I started to wonder, where did my pet go? Where is she/he now? Do animals have a soul? Will they come back? These are all the questions I asked when I lost my rabbit Bello suddenly and unexpectedly. Because I felt this could not be it, that there was unfinished business and more lessons to learn, I had a deep longing for Bello, to connect with him, to hug him. I did not feel a resolution in our relationship. I missed him and needed to have answers.

So, I went on Google and found an animal communicator, Trisha, who lived in Perth and could talk to animals after they pass away. I called her immediately and explained to her what had happened and that there

ANIMAL CONNECTION

were unresolved issues. I needed to connect with Bello. I booked an appointment, sent her Bello's photograph, and it all started from there. My journey and my path in life changed from that moment as I started learning and exploring more and more about animals.

In this chapter, I aim to answer via my own intuition and inner guidance some common questions I hear, such as:

- Do animals have a soul?
- Where do animals go after they pass away?
- Can humans incarnate into animals and vice versa?

In short, the answer to each question is yes.

In this chapter, I take the opportunity to be the voice of the animals and a channel for them. I also wish to share their message that they are here on a journey just like we are, with their own unique path and purpose. They also have lessons to learn, experiences they want to have. Most of all, they want to be either a mirror for us or our spiritual teacher or guide, or simply to hold space for us and be our loving companion, friend, and channel or messenger.

Animals teach us so much through the way they reflect us. They do say animals start to look and behave like their owners after a time. We learn from their behavior, their energy, their movement, their communication. They can also pick up on our illnesses and diseases and take them on as their own. For example, I suffer from digestion problems, and my rabbit Isabel, with whom I spent five years, also suffered from the same problem. When I got Isabel, I was healing from stomach pain, and so I spent many hours with her, talking to her about my problems and sharing with her my pain.

When Trisha told me what my rabbits shared with her, I realized I was not alone, that I was not imagining things. There is so much more to animals than most humans know.

I grew up with animals from the age of three. So, for me, animal communication is second nature. Most of my lessons have come from the loss of pet animals and from observing their behavior. I can spend all day, every day, watching my rabbits, their every move, every pose.

I have been observing my rabbits at home, and their daily routine is pretty much the same each day. They eat, exercise, play, and sleep, and they repeat this every three hours. After each exercise, they eat, and then they take a deep rest to recoup their energy. They have a balanced life compared to many humans. They spend hours meditating. After each rest, they yawn and do some stretching and yoga before they go to eat and exercise. Many yoga poses have come from the rabbit's natural movements.

Rabbits have strong base chakras and teach us about stability, grounding, rebirth, and procreation. They also teach us stillness and peace. I learned to meditate with my rabbits, especially my rabbit Bello. Rabbits are also very closely connected to their divinity. They have a strong crown and third-eye chakra. I used to watch my rabbit Bello when he was meditating, and I often found him staring up at the sky. I realized he had a strong connection to the cosmos, like me. Maybe we both came from the same star or galaxy. This is what got me further interested in animals and their souls' origin and their connection to humans.

My belief about life is that we can reincarnate in different forms, as a human or an animal, and can come from the same source and share the same soul group. We can have in our soul group or star family group a combination of animals and humans. For example, a pet may keep reincarnating back to you. In one life, this pet may have been your beloved grandmother, sister, brother, or past lover. It is so important to recognize and appreciate this and show respect to both animals and humans equally and learn to communicate with animals. We are both clairsentient beings. Animals have much more developed senses than humans. Some can fly; humans cannot fly. Some can live underwater; humans cannot. They have a very strong sense of smell, hearing, and feeling. Animals have many gifts that we humans don't have. They are here on their own journey to experience their life, fulfill their own purpose, and learn their own life lessons. So, let's work on this together with them. They are here to help and guide us, and we are here to help and guide them. So much healing and magic happens when you share this journey with animals.

Today I purchased a new car. As it is the first time that I have purchased a brand-new car from a showroom I feel very happy and proud of my achievement.

In the evening, I parked my car in our underground parking lot. This morning I came to the car and found a huge bird poop in the middle of the windscreen. I looked up and saw a pigeon sitting there at peace. I said hello to the pigeon.

They say it's good luck when pigeons (birds in general) poop on you. So, I said thank you to the pigeon for wishing me good luck. In Christian and Jewish symbolism, pigeons symbolize purity, simplicity, peace, hope, and happiness.[25]

Pigeons have made important contributions to humanity, especially in times of war when homing pigeons were put to use as messengers. These so-called war pigeons carried many vital messages, and some have been decorated for their services.

When I was a little girl, I used to love playing and communicating with the pigeons, and I still do now. I communicate to all living beings that come across my path.

---

25 https://dreamingandsleeping.com/pigeon-dove-spirit-animalsymbolism-and-meaning/

10

SILENT LANGUAGE

"Until one has loved an animal, a part
of one's soul remains unawakened."

— Anatole France

The oldest universal language is that of telepathy. The word "telepathy" comes from the Greek *tele*, meaning "distant" and *patheia* meaning "feeling, perception, passion, and experience."

If you observe how nature communicates, you will see that animals, plants, planets, oceans, and humans all communicate in the same way — through the vibration of sound and voice, through pictures and visualization, through emotions and touch, through smell and a combination of these. We have so many senses that enable us to live on this planet. If we use them properly, these senses bring survival and success.

Each species has its own unique combination of the above, and humans also have certain gifts or strengths. For example, I am a kinesthetic human being — so, for me, emotions, feelings, touch, and smell are my strengths, followed by pictures, visualization, and voice.

You may have heard about the 4Cs: clairvoyance, clairsentience, clairaudience, claircognizance. When we were babies and children, this was how we communicated to our mother and father, and to animals. This is why children often have a very good connection with animals.

As we get older, we start school, we get conditioned, and these abilities dim. So, we start using language as our primary communication method.

I spent my childhood with animals, especially rabbits. We had about twenty rabbits. I used to sit with them, talk to them, make them carrot juice and vegetable soup, and sometimes I would sit with them on the grass and eat plants like them, walk like them, and make facial expressions like them. One time at school, my teacher noticed that I was making funny facial expressions, moving my nose like a rabbit, and addressed this issue with my father. My father said, "Oh, that's because she spends a lot of time with rabbits."

The truth is, I did not only think and behave like a rabbit. I had past lives as a rabbit, so I felt very comfortable with their companionship.

Animals teach us how to live in the NOW. This was one of my biggest lessons after unexpectedly losing my rabbit Bello and my lovebird Mina. I remember saying, "Next weekend we will do this … next weekend I will play with you more … next week I will take you outside." What hurt me the most about the loss is that "next weekend" never came. I never got the opportunity to do all the things that I planned to do with my animals. Their lives are much shorter than humans, and we never know how long they will be with us. It took my losing a few of my pets to realize the importance of living in the moment and enjoying time with our loved ones when they are still with us. The importance of being present with our loved ones really is the present of our lives.

I remember when I lost my white rabbit, Bello. I was going on holiday to Queensland and decided to give

Bello to a friend to look after. When I came back from holiday, I waited a few more days to pick up Bello. It was Monday morning, 10 February 2017 when I told my friend I was coming to pick up Bello. I then got a message from my friend that he had found Bello dead on the floor overnight, just after 3 am. He sent photos to my phone. I could not believe my ears or my eyes. I was in total shock and disbelief. The whole situation was surreal.

We buried Bello and did a ceremony for him the following day. I was hurting and grieving and needed answers. I did a Google search for an animal communicator who could connect with Bello. I needed to know what had happened and why he had left me so suddenly and so young.

I found the details of Trisha, the animal communicator, and called her. She was immediately available to take my call, and I booked a reading with her. She asked me to send her a photo of Bello.

A few days later, Trisha called me with the reading for Bello after she had established a connection with him. She told me Bello was a special soul, a special rabbit. He was angelic. The planet was too harsh for him, the energy too dense; he was too sensitive and so could not stay here long. His message and purpose were for me to connect with the afterlife and to reconnect me with the animal communication gift that I have.

I used to sing a song to Bello. It is in the Macedonian language, and it's basically one sentence. I sang it over and over because when I sing to my pets, it helps me to connect to them.

> *Bello Bello Bello kako sneg,*
> *Bello kako sneg,*
> *Bello kako sneg.*

It means *Bello, Bello, white like snow, white like snow, white like snow.* In the Macedonian language, Belo means white, and in Italian, Bello means beautiful boy. So, my Bello meant "white beautiful boy."

A few weeks later, my other rabbit Smoki, Bello's best friend, also passed away and joined Bello over the rainbow bridge.

I contacted Trisha again for another reading. Trisha helped me get through my grief and get a better understanding of what happens to animals after they die.

FREE YOUR MIND, LISTEN WITH YOUR HEART

I lost a few other rabbits after that, and so I started a practice of doing ceremonies for them and getting paintings done of them.

I also lost my lovebird, Mina. The loss, grief, and trauma I experienced from losing Mina almost tipped me over to the other side. The pain of the depression was strong. But staying there in that state was a far greater pain than the pain of moving forward and making changes in my life. I needed to let go of the fear. I needed to live in the moment and spend time with my loved ones while I still had them, in the here and now.

I had had Mina for only three weeks before she found a way out of the cage when she was outside and flew to the big tree in the neighbor's house, where she was attacked by a crow.

Five minutes earlier, I had said to Mina, "I am just going to the pet shop to buy something and when I come back, I will let you fly around the house and play with you."

I went upstairs to get ready to leave the house, and I went outside to check on Mina. I saw her standing on top of her cage. She seemed happy and relaxed, chirping and being curious about her new environment.

She spent about five minutes in the backyard, exploring, and I thought she would come inside the house. Instead, she chirped one last time like she was saying goodbye and flew to the tree, and then onto another tree in the neighbor's house and then toward the big, tall tree in another neighboring house, where crows usually nest.

This was the third time now I was making plans with my animals, telling them "next weekend when I am not working, I will spend time with you, I will do this, I will do that …" and those moments never came. I was always too busy working long hours and not dedicating enough time to my animals.

So, in February of 2020, when I left my job, and then the COVID situation started, I spent six months, every single day, with my pets. I did not waste another moment. I enjoyed my time with them, so at least when it's time for them to leave, I can say: I did my best. I enjoyed them while they were here and made many happy memories with them.

I am not going to waste another moment thinking about the things I want or making plans about what I want to do. I will just do it!

I opened my wings. I started to fly again and take courageous steps in my life. I traveled to Italy on a yoga retreat in the mountains. I bought a guitar. I started writing songs and poems. I started singing, dancing, and just enjoying my life in the comfort of my home with my favorite beings, my pets. I was enjoying each day like it was my last, going to bed, feeling peace, knowing I had done my best for that day. Breathing each breath fully, expanding my chest, watching my belly rise, listening to my exhaling, like it was my last breath. Living in the now is what brings feelings of happiness, peace, and freedom. There are no anxious or fearful thoughts about the future; it's just me and this moment together as one.

During the times I was going through grief over the loss of my pets, I also got some assistance through coaching and counseling. I was referred to Elizabeth Kubler Ross's 7 Stages of Grief model. By reading about the 7 stages of grief, I started to understand better what I was experiencing and how I could move through the stages quicker and with more ease. Just having an awareness of the different stages of grief helped me cope with difficult times. It helped knowing it was just a stage, a phase; it would pass, and things would get better.

The 7 stages of grief are:

- Shock and denial — this is a state of disbelief and numbed feelings
- Pain and guilt
- Anger and bargaining
- Depression
- The upward turn
- Reconstruction and working through
- Acceptance and hope

11

LIFE BETWEEN LIVES OR "LBL"

Friday 14th August 2020

After reading the book *Journey of Souls* by Dr. Michael Newton, I went onto the Newton Institute website to find a practitioner who could perform a life-between-lives (LBL) session for me. This is a session where you connect to your soul and guides and ask any questions you have about your soul journey.

I was specifically looking to connect to my guides and the Wise Council of Elders to get information about my life purpose with animals, my deep connection to animals, and information on past lives I have experienced as an animal.

I contacted a few therapists, and Melissa from Melbourne was the first one to reply. She called me on the same day, and I decided to book a session with her. When choosing people to work with, I usually observe the signs to get a feeling about whether I am on the right path. For example, I noticed that when I received the booking form in my email inbox, I clicked on the "I accept" button at exactly 1:11 pm. This was confirmation that I was on the right path, so I proceeded to make the payment and have the session.

The session was booked for a few days later, on Thursday 20th August 2020.

Animal Akashic Records

A day before my LBL session, I was guided to an animal Akashic Records online course facilitated by Tamra Oviatt.

The first thing to appear was my power animal: a tiger with a message to keep going on my path. It told me I was powerful and strong and to keep following my path with courage and avoid distractions.

Then appeared the owl, followed by the peacock, and the message was to focus on my work, speak less, and express more through color and creativity than speech.

LIFE BETWEEN LIVES OR "LBL"

After the power animal exercise, I was guided to my animal cards, which are messages from your animal spirit guide oracle cards by Steven Farmer. I picked three cards and got the unicorn, humpback whale, and walrus. As I was reading my cards, the group on the online course started sharing, and many of them had also got the unicorn as their power animal.

The teacher then said that hers was a whale, and the whale is the guardian of the animal Akashic Records. Coincidentally, I also picked the whale card in my deck, so I read and accepted the message, which was about connection with music, singing, and sound healing.

Yesterday, my gift arrived in the post, a steel drum or moonsun, that I ordered a few weeks ago. I spent the evening playing this drum, and it brought me so much joy, connecting me more to my animals as I played the drum to them.

The next day, after having had the activation for animal Akashic Records, I had my LBL session. I was so intrigued to see what I would experience.

I started my LBL session with Melissa at 10:30 am.

After we had a brief chat, I closed my eyes, and within 30 seconds I felt myself sinking deeper and deeper into my soul. Layer after layer, colors started changing until I found myself in the womb of an animal. I was being born as a rabbit. I experienced the birth, which was very quick, and then found myself amongst a collective of rabbits. There were hundreds or maybe thousands of white rabbits together in a forest. At the same time, our forest was being populated with humans. They arrived on a ship and started building houses on the land. They used the rabbits as feed. The rabbits were also used to eat the plants and work the land (digging and making it fertile) for the humans to grow their food. There was a group of rabbits used as feed, a group of rabbits helping with the land, and another group of rabbits, which is where I was, whose role was to infuse the planet with the energy of grounding, stability, fertility, safety, and unconditional love.

After this life, again I was born as a rabbit but in this life, I had an independent life as a rabbit, not as a collective. I felt myself running around free in the forest until I encountered humans. For the second part of my life, I was living in close contact with humans.

I then experienced a third life. I was in the womb of a human mother in the land of Africa. My African mother died after my birth, and a white English lady who traveled the world on a wooden ship adopted me. I spent my childhood on the ship and had a pet cat. A war started, and the ship was attacked and caught fire. My parents died. I managed to escape with another girl. We were about 15, and we settled in a desert near Egypt, I believe. In this life, I traveled the desert, teaching some religious studies, and I ran an orphanage.

In the second part of the session, after I experienced three past lives, my therapist Melissa started asking me questions about my connection to animals and why I was here on Planet Earth — what my purpose was.

I started explaining that my soul was able to be human and animal at the same time. I can come in different forms and sizes, with different variants of light and consciousness, and experience more than one form at once. I can come on the planet incarnated as a human but also an animal at the same time. Only the more advanced souls have this ability to share or split their light and consciousness into more than one body or vessel.

My soul is part of a collective of lightworker engineers, and my soul group is involved with designing and engineering the animal species, getting them ready to come to the planet. When I am not incarnated on the planet,

I am helping other souls to incarnate on the planet in a group, either as an animal group or a human group. I work with one or two types of soul groups at a time.

I help other souls to incarnate, but I also act as a life review counselor and work with souls who return to the afterlife with a review of their lives and their lessons. This was also confirmed in a reading I had of my Akashic Records about six months ago, which I talk about in my first book.

My other role is to help the design and engineering of animal groups coming onto the planet for a different purpose. There are many souls like me, known as soul engineers. Again, this was confirmed to me in an Akashic Record reading I had six months ago, which I talk about in my first book. It was in the soul-realignment studies, which focus on humans only, that I learned I had the ability to come as an animal and a human, because my role as a soul engineer is so advanced that I can engineer a whole group of animals to come to the planet, such as turtles, rabbits, and some forms of birds and parrots. This explains my close connection to birds and rabbits. I have had pet parrots and rabbits since I was three years old.

Moving on from this, during my LBL session, I also learned about the different colors of our souls. I was a reddish or blood-orange colored soul who could split into other souls colored blue. These blue souls can be a group of animals or a group of humans. New souls are usually white. As they experience life as a human or animal, they get colors depending on what their life purpose and life lessons are. If their lesson, for example, is about being grounded, safe and primal, they have the color red. If they came to live a life from a heart space and experience life as unconditional love with compassion, they are usually pink souls, and green souls are those who stay to experience life as a human-angel hybrid. They usually stay close to family members or a person they were very close to. They choose not to ascend to be reincarnated, but to stay as a guide or angelic support for family members or friends they were close to.

But some souls, especially the new souls, haven't yet mastered how to leave the body and ascend and may not have a body light enough to rise. These souls may still have attachments to people, to land, to a house, or something else they were very close to, and they may also have some unresolved emotional trauma that is weighing them down. These souls usually find someone in the physical realm who is very sensitive or a psychic medium who can help them resolve their unresolved issues and therefore help them back to the light. It is commonly known that cats play this role as well.

Cats assist souls who, for example, are attached to their house or land, to leave and go toward the light. Cats are often used as guides to humans, and they help clear the energies of a house or block of land where there is unresolved trauma arising from wars, murder scenes, etc. Some cats, or even dogs, may also come as a reincarnation of a family member or a friend who has passed away, and be a companion to the person they have the unresolved emotional trauma with, and/or they are there as guides to help them learn life lessons. These lessons are often related to compassion, discipline, rescue, abandonment, and love. Often you feel this when you rescue an abandoned or a hurt animal — you have this feeling, this inner knowing that this animal is here to teach you lessons, that it may be an incarnation of someone who has recently passed away. I am getting goosebumps as I write this and look at the time. It is 1:13 pm, so this is my confirmation I am on the right path. When I started writing this chapter of the book, the time was 12:12 pm; this is double confirmation that I am sharing the correct information.

12

SHAMANIC JOURNEY

1st April 2021

Today I visited a wellness center in Dubai called Miracles and experienced a one-hour shamanic session with Indrani. I did this after losing my rabbit soul mate, my dearest Isabel.

When I left Melbourne in August 2020 for Dubai, I planned to bring Isabel over later, perhaps a year later after I was settled in Dubai.

But on 24th February 2021, I heard that Isabel had passed away. I was devastated. I wanted to learn why she had left so early and what would happen next in our journey.

During this session, I wanted guidance from my soul as to previous life incarnations I had had. So, I entered the space, switched off my mind, and started my meditation to elevate to the higher realms. I felt myself elevating. Firstly, I touched the tips of some high mountains. As I rose higher over lakes and mountains, above the clouds, and into the ether and the cosmos, I saw the world from above.

Here I was greeted by two figures from a distance. One was white, one was dark gray. The white figure was a female with long white hair. She approached me and came to my left side. The dark figure was a masculine figure standing on the right. When the light female figure approached me, she transformed a few times into different forms. I saw different animals, colors, and wings. She was showing me that she was a transformational-type soul. She told me she was my soul sister. I recognized her, and we hugged.

In the first life revealed to me, I was a white cat living in a wooden cottage in a forest with an old lady. We had a very close relationship. I saw a wooden door with an arch, and we were going in and out of this door together. We were soulmates. I was her guide in that life. The old lady passed away, with me in her arms, and then shortly afterwards, I passed away. In that life, I wanted to experience human love and contact with a human.

In the second life, I was a big black bird with large piercing eyes. I was flying over lakes and mountains. It was a beautiful place. I could see some snow on the top of the mountains, lots of greenery, and rivers on the ground. In this life, I wanted to experience freedom, balance, independence, and courage.

In the third life, I was a cow, a very happy cow. I was living in a garden on a small family farm. I enjoyed lying on the grass, being in nature surrounded by plants and flowers. This experience gave me lessons in being grounded close to Earth and nature, stability, and security.

In the last life, I was a rabbit, a wild rabbit. I saw myself being born as a baby rabbit. I was in a family of rabbits and then I went off on my own. I met another rabbit on the way, and we became best friends. I enjoyed running in endless green fields. I wanted to experience freedom, stability, grounding, and fear. I came to Planet Earth to feel and experience the emotions of fear and freedom.

When we finished, I thanked the guides, hugged my soul sister, and left, coming back to myself. Indrani asked me who I thought that female guide was. I said, "In the end when we hugged, I realized it was Isabel." I felt so much love and peace from this session.

13

FINDING MY INNER ARTIST

After Bello passed away, I wanted to paint a picture of him. So, I joined an adult art class in Melbourne called "Life with Paint." It was a two-hour class one evening after work and was a big thing for me because I had not done any art since I was in primary school.

My mother is naturally talented in art and all things creative. She has magical healing hands as well. I also remember watching my cousin Aneta, who is the daughter of my mum's twin sister. When we spent time together in our childhood, she always drew beautiful portraits of women. I used to wish I could have her talent. I decided to search for my own talent within.

During this class, in which we were to paint a cockatoo parrot, I found my hidden gift for art and creativity.

FREE YOUR MIND, LISTEN WITH YOUR HEART

I say this because my painting looked totally different from everyone else's, and I finished it rapidly. Once I put the brush onto the canvas, I started painting like a born artist. Everyone else was painting a white cockatoo parrot; I was doing my own thing, at my own pace. I painted a very colorful bird that looked like a baby parrot.

Two years later, I manifested this bird in my life, and along came my conure parrot Gucci who brought me so much love and joy. I did not plan to buy a parrot, but when I saw him at the pet shop, it was love at first sight.

I attended three more classes at Life with Paint, continuing to paint my own versions of the picture that we were guided to paint.

My second guided painting was a turtle; it was a happy, smiling turtle.

The turtle spirit animal is one of the oldest living animals in the world. You can gain much wisdom from turtle symbolism, such as persistence, endurance, and longevity. It tells you it's time to slow down, travel light, and go at your own pace. This is what you should be doing with your life when things start to get overwhelming. The turtle symbolism teaches you that life is a never-ending series of arrivals.

You should not focus on missed opportunities but on where you want to be and how you are going to get there. Just keep moving toward your goals, no matter how slow or difficult the journey gets. You will get there! [26]

Then I painted a mum fox and baby fox, signifying unconditional love, and then finally a pink swan, which to me signified freedom. "Go and paint and follow your own path, my dear," this swan whispered to me.

After having four guided painting sessions, I painted my first freestyle painting of my rabbits Smoki and Bello, who recently crossed over the rainbow bridge.

July 2020

This week I got a spirit guide reading from Shelly, a soul-realignment practitioner in Melbourne.

She gave me information about the seven guides that I currently have. She explained most of them are with me for life. They are assigned to me only, but there is one who is with me for a specific project and mission. She gave me some fascinating information about my

---

26 https://trustedpsychicmediums.com/spirit-animals/turtle-spirit-animal/

seven guides; it resonated with me. A few days before the reading, I painted two of my guides intuitively. One was a beautiful angel in light pastel pink and blue colors. For about two days, I had a headache in the front of my head. It was a vision coming to me. When I converted the vision inside my head into a painting, my headache went away.

The other painting was a green painting, which I named Green Dancing Goddess. It was about connection to my heart. The color of the heart chakra is green. I also added a golden path to the painting. To me, this artwork was all about following the golden path of abundance through the connection of my heart.

Creating art and colors is an excellent tool for me to express my soul and my visions. I danced in front of my green goddess painting to infuse it with extra love and energy.

14

2020 AWAKENING OF HUMANITY

08.08.2020 — Lion's Gate Portal

This morning, Saturday, I woke up and called my nephew to wish him a happy birthday. He is 11 years old today. What a special number on this special day!

Shortly after that, I looked at the time. It was about to turn 11:11 am. I remembered that the Lion's Gate portal is opening today. What a perfect time to do meditation[27] to activate the gateway portal, awaken the layers of our DNA and activate and align our chakra system to receive an energy upgrade and the codes of our soul mission.

---

27   https://youtu.be/WptPc_OC3QU

FREE YOUR MIND, LISTEN WITH YOUR HEART

We receive extra light from this time from the superstar Sirius, which is much brighter than our sun. The extra light helps us exist in the COVID pandemic and deep dive into shadow work. We have been called to re-evaluate our lives. Are we in alignment with our career, our relationships, our body?[28]

Deep diving into our shadow work means concentrating on what needs to change in our lives.

The purpose of this light is to illuminate our hearts and allow our light to be stronger, brighter. It allows us to step into our personal power and do what we came here on this planet to do. Each person is unique; we all have our own golden path and purpose. And we follow this path at our own pace. No comparison, no competition with others is required. You will reach your destination if you have trust and faith.

After the meditation session, I did a personal meditation and made my own wishes and intentions for the world, which are love, peace, and abundance. I noticed my rabbit Lewis was also meditating, sitting peacefully

---

28 https://youtu.be/L8Um7jTBfQ8

under my chair whilst I was doing this work. My rabbits Isabel and Pepe, who were also in the room, were also in a meditation position and state.

After the meditation, I painted a canvas, starting with the colors pink and silver as a base, followed by a red serpent for the feminine and blue for the masculine, intertwining them together, then blending all the colors to create unity and oneness. I then danced in front of the painting to infuse some more love into it.

When you buy a painting, it's not just a painting; you also receive a piece of the creator's soul, infused with the energy with which it was created. The magic and power of creating art are incredible. Creating beautiful things is medicine for our hearts and souls.

To add to the flow and synchronicity, I pulled a card from the Archangel Power Tarot Cards by Doreen Virtue, and I got the King of Raphael card, which is all about trust and the ability to accomplish great things. It also says to indulge any longing I may have to create art or music. It is exactly what I am doing today. I also have a passion to start singing, and I am learning how to play the guitar.

FREE YOUR MIND, LISTEN WITH YOUR HEART

Winter Solstice and the Great Conjunction: 21st December

December 21 marks the Winter Solstice in the northern hemisphere, which is the shortest day and longest night of the year. It is also when the sun is at its lowest daily maximum elevation. The exact opposite happens in the southern hemisphere today, where it is called the December Solstice or Summer Solstice. The Great Conjunction occurs when Jupiter and Saturn align from the perspective of the Earth. This vibrant planetary conjunction is also referred to as the "Christmas Star."

What is the Great Conjunction?
According to Henry Throop, an astronomer at NASA, "You can imagine the solar system to be a racetrack, with each of the planets as a runner in their own lane and the Earth toward the center of the stadium. From our vantage point, we'll be able to see Jupiter on the inside lane, approaching Saturn all month and finally overtaking it on December 21."

The planets regularly pass each other in the solar system. The positions of Jupiter and Saturn are aligned in the sky about once every twenty years. But this year's celestial spectacle is especially rare for a few reasons — it has been nearly 400 years since both the planets passed this close to each other in the sky. The last time it happened was in 1623, thirteen years after Galileo Galilei built his first telescope. This is when it was given the name "The Great Conjunction."[29]

To celebrate the Winter Solstice and Great Conjunction, we had an online meditation circle with my teacher Apostolia in Greece, joined by other members of the group from the happiness retreat circle I am part of. Together we did some breathing exercises. We then let go of what was no longer serving us by writing it on a piece of paper and burning it, then burying the ashes in the ground for re-birth. We created new intentions for the year 2021 whilst singing and dancing. It was a very beautiful and memorable event.

---

29 https://gadgets.ndtv.com/science/news/winter-solstice-great-conjunction-saturn-jupiter-meet-december-21-2020-how-to-watch-2341630

15

ANCESTRAL HEALING

November 2020

This month I started an ancestral healing course with Bridget Nielsen. I have been doing a lot of reading about ancestral healing over the last few years and have been practicing honoring my ancestors in many ways. I have an altar in my house where I place fresh flowers and light candles every week.

The time of Halloween is known as the "thinning of the veil." The thinning makes it easier to connect with our beloved ones and ancestors.

In Macedonia, where I grew up, it's part of our cultural tradition to honor our ancestors. When we go to Church, we always light candles for our crossed-over ancestors and when a loved one passes over, we observe a forty-day period in which we honor the spirit by having a candle burning, along with some food and water as an offering to the spirit. We believe that the spirit stays around us for forty days before it moves on and transcends to another form.

As part of the ancestral healing course, we started by creating an altar. In that altar, we placed all the things that we intuitively pick up that resonate with our ancestors.

We did various exercises to connect to our ancestors. My favorite one was a blood-and-bone exercise that clears and heals the stored DNA ancestral trauma we carry that is not serving us, causing us pain and discomfort, or feels burdensome in our body. After doing this exercise, which lasted about 70 minutes, I went for a swim in the sea to wash away any left-over negative energy. Swimming in the sea is one of the best medicines for our body and soul. I felt so much lighter, healthier, and more refreshed.

I then treated myself to a delicious dinner, sitting outside listening to the sounds of water and watching the new moon in the sky — a time to mark new beginnings and set new intentions for the week, month, and rest of the year.

ANCESTRAL HEALING

Another favorite exercise of mine is to connect to the various groups of my ancestral lineage, even with those I don't consciously know.

One of the soul groups that came to me was the animal group. When I connected to the animal soul group of ancestors, I felt warmth in my body and my heart; I felt grounded and safe. I felt loved and supported by this group, which I connected to by writing on a piece of paper and stepping on it. But I did not know which one I was stepping on. I was guided by what I was feeling, and my strongest connection was to the animal soul group, which also needs healing, just like humans do.

Animals, like humans, incarnate by choice and free will to experience their own unique journey, learn their own lessons, or teach humans lessons. Many animals travel with a specific person or group family and incarnate several times throughout the same life of a human. This is demonstrated through my own experience with my rabbit Lewis, who was previously my rabbit Leo. When I moved from Auckland to Sydney, Leo traveled with me on the plane, but when I moved from Sydney to London, I did not take Leo with me, and a few years later he passed away in Melbourne. Lewis was born in Melbourne a few years after that, and when I moved from Melbourne to Dubai, Lewis came with me. He will always be with me. He is my teacher and my best friend. We have shared many lives in the past as well.

I always felt very sad that I did not bring Leo with me to London, so when he came back into my life, I decided I would not part ways with him again. I used the animal communicator that I work with, Trisha, to help me and Lewis along the way. Trisha connected with Lewis back in Australia while I was in Dubai waiting for him, and she explained to him what was going on and what to expect. She then communicated back to me throughout the flight. I am happy to share that the flight from Melbourne to Dubai was a success. Lewis arrived safe and sound, and he was back to himself only a few hours later. I am so happy that I used Trisha to assist us with the process, and I am over the moon to have Lewis with me here in Dubai.

16

MY PERSONAL GUIDE TO FREEDOM

We are on a path to personal and universal freedom, breaking free from systems and structures that no longer serve humanity, breaking free from authority, slavery, and control, and breaking free from illusion and the veil between us as a human body and us as divine spiritual beings.

Everyone will have their own meaning and definition of freedom.

For me, it is about connecting to my soul and higher self, my life purpose, the reasons I incarnated, what I am here to accomplish, and what lessons I am here to learn. Knowing I am on the right path and doing what I came here to do gives me the peace and freedom to express myself, express my heart and soul, and express my creativity through all the many gifts and channels available to me.

Freedom for me is knowing that once I fulfill my mission here on Earth, balance all my karma, experience all the things I want to experience, and learn all and complete my lessons, I can choose to have a "holiday" life and come back as another being, such as an animal. I often tell my rabbits, Lewis and Isabel, that in my next life, I am taking a holiday and coming back as a rabbit, a wild rabbit, where I can be in nature and run around free. I want to explore the world free like a rabbit. I think this life will suit me very well.

I see men or the masculine as the structure and women or the feminine as the glue that holds the structure together. To me, this is equality. The blend of the yin and yang. The balance between yin and yang. Equality for me is not about women needing to prove they can do the same things as men, or be as physically strong as men, because in that case we would also expect men to be emotionally as strong as women or as intuitive, or to be able to bear children like women can.

Equality in men and women is to understand the differences between the two and fully embrace the differences in the understanding that both poles are required to create equality or balance. So we need the physical strength and discipline of the masculine, and we need the light, softness, gentleness, and vulnerability of the feminine. Blended, we create balance or equality.

One other meaning of freedom for me is the freedom from burdening or difficult thoughts so that I can find a clear space in my head and be in the now, free from any thoughts, just enjoying being and feeling my body, my breath, my environment, nature, and listening to the sounds of nature.

This, for me, is the ultimate freedom.

How to achieve this?

It is a journey to finding freedom. I talk about finding inner peace in my first book through the yoga and meditation retreats I did over the last five years. Finding inner peace is the first step to finding freedom. You must rid yourself of negative or burdening thoughts that affect your emotions.

How to do that? Here are some suggestions.

- Observe your thoughts, let them come and go, practice mindfulness.
- Are they reoccurring thoughts or different thoughts?
- If they are reoccurring thoughts, ask yourself:
  - Why am I having these thoughts every day?
  - What emotions or life experiences have I not dealt with in my life?
  - What burdening thoughts are occupying my headspace and taking up my emotions?

Sometimes you will visualize the events if you are a visual person, or you will feel the emotions and memories from these events if you are more of a kinesthetic person. I am both, so I will address these.

Sometimes, they are memories from past lives. I have many of these. I often experience memories of my soul from past lives through my emotions. The more emotionally connected you are, the more you can experience and regress to your past lives.

- Is there anything I need to heal from past lives?
- What do I need to heal from this life?
- How can I shed light on these events and memories?

- What things have I not said or expressed that are still burdening me?
- Do I need to forgive someone or something?
- What things have I not acted on but have thought about constantly? Am I feeling stagnate? Is fear settling in and disabling me from making decisions and moving forward into actions? If yes, explore fear emotions and trapped trauma from the past.

I have used various healing modalities to heal my trauma, which I talk about in my first book. If you are reading this book but haven't yet read my first book, I encourage you to read my first book and then return to this one. Trauma can be from this life or past lives. Ancestral trauma is transferred to you down your ancestral lineage. Healing this trauma takes time. It's very important that you have chosen to incarnate again in your chosen body. Explore why. What do you need to heal? What lessons do you need to learn? How is the trauma showing up in your life? It can be a physical dis-ease or illness, a repeated strain or injury, a thinking pattern, or repeated behavior that is not serving you.

- Are you listening to your body? What is your body trying to express to you via aches and pains or chronic dis-ease? These are messages from your soul sent to your body asking you to address the issues on a deeper level. As I learned in the psychosomatic therapy course, "The issues are in your tissues," and your body is talking to you. Are you listening?

- When you are at work, are you working, or are you thinking about something else?
- Do you enjoy your work?
- Do you find passion, meaning, and purpose in your work?
- Are you waiting for the time to pass by so you can go home? How many minutes or hours are you spending at work thinking about this?
- Where would you rather be?
- What would you be rather doing?
- How many hours per day would you rather be working?
- Do your beliefs serve you and set you free?
- Does your religion serve you positively and set you free?
- Are you present?
- Are you living and being in the now?

Focus on your breath and the moment currently in front of you. Breathe deeply, open your hearing, open your senses, feel and hear.

When you have expressed each day what you want to express, and you have done the things you wanted to do and taken the action you wanted to take, this is when you can go to sleep or have an evening rest or meditation and say to yourself, *I did it.*

- I lived a day how I wanted to live it.
- I said what I wanted to say.
- I expressed what I wanted to express.
- I took the action I wanted to take.

Now breathe. Breathe deeply. Feel the breath in your belly, in your heart. Put your hand on your belly and breathe in that space, then put your hand on your heart and breathe in that space. Repeat until you find the feeling of peace and you feel clear.

And pat yourself on the back. Acknowledge yourself. Give gratitude to yourself. Give love and appreciation to yourself. Maybe even hug yourself. Take the time to feel the emotions of gratitude, love, and appreciation.

Your burdening and negative thoughts should now disappear. You will have a clear head, you will feel rested and at peace, and this is when you find freedom and joy within. When you find joy, you dance, you sing, you play, you paint, you write, you create, you are alive! You feel alive! And this is freedom.

Freedom is also knowing you have no attachments. And this includes attachments to your own body. I came into the world with bare hands; I will leave with bare hands.

One thing I did gain in this lifetime is the memories and the imprints in my soul. All that matters is to have good, happy memories and positive imprints on the soul. One day, my body will be gifted back to nature and buried in Mother Earth. However, my soul will keep going. It will keep traveling, keep transforming. My soul is immortal. So, I place importance on taking care of my soul, my soul memories, and soul imprints. Learning about my soul and doing my healing work is how I take care of my soul.

If you live every day like this and repeat the same process, it will become your habit, your pattern, and life will be good! What you cannot do today, you will do tomorrow. The key is taking each day as it comes and living in the now. A lot can happen in a day. Just one day is all you need to start a new cycle, a new habit, a new pattern.

17

NEW MOON, NEW CYCLE, NEW EARTH

15th October 20

I joined a New Moon Circle online with my teacher Apostolia in Athens.

We started with some breathing and stretching exercises, journaling our intentions, sharing, and singing while Apostolia played her guitar.

I had been struggling some with forgiveness over the past year, and during the two-hour session with Apostolia and the group, I felt my heart opening and a small stone falling out. It was the forgiveness. I was finally ready to forgive and let go of what I was holding in my heart and not serving me anymore.

FREE YOUR MIND, LISTEN WITH YOUR HEART

> *"If we really want to love we must learn how to forgive."*
>
> — Mother Teresa[30]

According to the Chinese calendar, every sixty years marks a new cycle, with a turning point and new beginnings. The year 2020 is that year. "2020 offers us a chance to repair the damage we have caused, reconcile our differences, and move forward in a more inclusive and sustainable way."

In terms of humanity, business leader Alex Liu says,

> *"There is a bigger picture we need to strive for, and anger — while a useful fuel — isn't a viable long-term strategy. But hope and connection are. We are 99.9 percent identical in our genetic makeup. We all know what it is to love and to grieve. And we've already seen what we're capable of when it really, truly, matters. We build hospitals in days. We move entire workforces and business models online. We collaborate on a global scale to share expertise and*

---

30   https://www.biography.com/religious-figure/mother-teresa

go after new solutions. There will be great joy in achieving true justice and equity."[31]

Alex Liu also says that it is a chance to right the wrongs, reconcile and reckon:

"... maybe the ancients were onto something, the universe is speaking to us, and there's a reason why we landed this throw of the dice. Maybe the next 60 years are our chance to right some of the wrongs, to reconcile and reckon. This is a moment that we must meet, and all such moments determine how we look at ourselves. What type of world do we want to leave behind us? What type of world do we want our children and theirs to inherit?"

He further says:

"There's a magnitude and mysticism about the number 60 that threads through many cultures. It's right there in the origin of mathematics with the ancient Sumerians and Babylonians. Related to that, it's how we measure the passing

---

31 https://www.weforum.org/agenda/2020/10/this-business-leader-says-2020-is-the-year-that-could-save-us/

of time — 60 seconds in a minute, 60 minutes in an hour."

The year 2020 was the year of global awakening: a New Earth is being reborn. Many souls are leaving due to COVID-19 deaths. New souls are incarnating. Many new children are being born who are coming here with a mission, a purpose, higher vibrations, more sensitivity, indigo, crystal, and rainbow children, old wise souls. It is important for parents to know this and educate themselves on how to parent these children consciously.

I remember when I was a child, my father always gave me choices and responsibility. He would give me money and ask me to go to the shops to buy things, then teach me about giving and receiving the correct change and honesty. I remember when I was 11 years old and my father was planning our relocation from Macedonia to Auckland, New Zealand. He asked my sister and me if we wanted to move there. He showed us on the map where it was and explained some details about it. Both my sister and I were excited about the opportunity and agreed. My parents treated us with respect since we were very young. They allowed their children to make their own choices in life, for which I am very grateful.

NEW MOON, NEW CYCLE, NEW EARTH

Today I had a discussion with a financial advisor, who shared with me his work and his passion for helping people save money, primarily for retirement or a rainy day. This got me thinking. Until the age of 25, I also had a narrow traditional view about money and saving money for the future. I got my first part-time job when I was only 14 and a half; I purchased my first car at the age of 15 when I got my driving license; my own brand-new apartment at the age of 18. I sold my first apartment and built a three-bedroom brand-new house at the age of 22. I then sold the house and made a profit, which I used to travel back to Europe and pay for my higher education in London. How did my parents contribute toward these goals? Simply by being there and my living with them in our family home. They never told me what to do or gave opinions about what I was doing. They were just there, present in my life. I made my own decisions and choices.

Now, fifteen years later, I have a different view of life and money. Now I give more importance to living in the now and being present in the moment. I practice appreciation of money and understand the money cycle — for example, the Japanese practice of making peace of your money known as "arigato your money." [32] Ken Honda

---

32 *Happy Money: The Japanese Art of Making Peace with Your Money*, Ken Honda

teaches how to treat money as a welcome guest, allowing it to come and go with respect and without resentment and embracing the process of giving money, not just receiving it.

I am always investing in myself, especially my education and life experiences, in writing my books and through my plan to one day open my own retreat and educational center. But first, I want to start with building an animal-rescue sanctuary. I have a great passion for the rescue of animals and teaching people about animals. My big dream is to have this animal sanctuary, which will also have rooms for music, yoga, dance, and art. This is what will support my children's life and their education.

The education system now is so old and outdated; it doesn't apply anymore to the modern world and the world our future children will be coming into. Our children are our future; they will bring new ideas, new concepts. They will come with their own source of abundance and creativity. Our role as adults or parents or teachers is to simply understand that and allow them to be. Learn and observe. Let them be their own creators of the life they want and came here to live. The same way I did, because my parents never instilled in me any specific ideas, beliefs, religions, what I should study, what job I should have, whom I should date, what

NEW MOON, NEW CYCLE, NEW EARTH

I should eat. They were silent on these matters, which left me to find my own boundaries, my own choices, learn my own lessons, find my own superpowers and gifts, and be responsible for my own life and decisions. This is the best gift they could have given me. Not the money they worked hard to save for twenty years to pay for the education I didn't want and a job that was their choice and not mine. The lessons I have learned about life from my parents and grandparents are the best gifts I have received along with all the animals I have shared my life with. My grandparents had a small farm near a small village in the mountains, where our family and friends came together on school holidays — the children to play with the goats, baby goats (kids), cows, pigs, and rabbits. We ate fresh goats cheese, drank fresh goats milk, eat homemade pasta and fresh vegetables from the garden, spent time in nature, eat cherries straight from the trees, and eat fresh walnuts from my grandparents' walnut tree.

Another thing I remember is my mother's presence and being surrounded by her creativity. She made many of my clothes, with my name as the label and other personalized marks. She knitted jumpers, scarves, pants, gloves, hats, and more. She made covers for our beds and tables. She made many crochets and crostiches, which were then framed and placed all around our home on the walls. I always felt love and warmth in our home, as most of these things were made by my mother, and she has such a natural talent.

These are my best childhood memories and my best life lessons. I take this opportunity to truly appreciate and fill my heart with gratitude to my parents, my grandparents, my uncles, my aunties, and all my ancestors. My mission is to continue this legacy. I want to give this opportunity and more to all other children out there. It's time for me to step into fulfilling my divine purpose and give back to humanity and our planet by working with animals, children, and parents, helping them on their journey to raising their vibrations and consciousness.

18

SPIRITUAL LAWS AND PRACTICES

There are many different spiritual laws, but the ones I find most practical are the spiritual laws by Vicent Guillem. I highly recommend reading his free e-book available on the link I provide here.

> *"The Spiritual Laws are a spiritual life guide, containing credible, authentic and reliable source of spiritual knowledge and wisdom. The author combines a profound scientific background with a humble, common-sense approach towards spirituality, full of truth and sentiment. He practices what he preaches, setting a model example by living his personal life according to the laws of love and free will."*[33]

---

33 http://thespirituallaws.blogspot.com

1st Law: The law of evolution

2nd Law: The law of free will

3rd Law: The law of spiritual justice

4th Law: The law of love

In my first book, *Unveiling the Path to Happiness*, I talk about the four agreements. I read a book by Don Miguel Ruiz, *The Four Agreements: A Practical Guide to Personal Freedom*, based on ancient Toltec wisdom. Reading this book about twelve years ago, I found it transformative and one of the first books that got me started on personal development and exploring spirituality. Practicing these simple agreements with myself has changed my life and given me more integrity and clarity. Once again, these four agreements are:[34]

1. **Be impeccable with your word.**
   It is about speaking with integrity. Say only what you mean and use the power of the spoken word in the direction of truth and love toward self and others.

---

34 https://lifeclub.org/books/the-fifth-agreement-don-miguel-ruiz-and-don-jose-ruiz-review-summary

2. **Don't take anything personally.**
   What people say and do is a projection of their own reality, not because of you. Be immune to the opinions and actions of others so that you are not the victim of needless suffering.
3. **Don't make assumptions.**
   Find the courage to ask questions and express yourself freely. Communicate clearly to avoid drama and misunderstanding.
4. **Always do your best.**
   Do your best, and let it improve and change. Avoid self-judgment, self-abuse, and regret.
   Now there is an extra agreement, and a new book called *The Fifth Agreement*, and this is:
5. **Be skeptical but learn to listen.**
   It is about using the power of doubt to question everything you hear, to listen to the intent behind the words to understand the real message.

19

THE PATH TO FREEDOM

In my first book, *Unveiling the Path to Happiness*, I share my personal journey and lessons to finding the path to peace through my own experiences and practices, led by my heart and intuition.

Here I will share some basic concepts I learned from Buddha's teachings, after my own inner awakening.

It's important to mention again that my learning in life does not come from books; it's already within me or I experience it, then I find the words for it and explanations in books, and then I have the aha moments and deeper understanding of what has been awakened in me through practice and experience.

"The Buddha" means the "Awakened One" or "Enlightened One."

Queen Māyā was the birth mother of Gautama Buddha, the sage on whose teachings Buddhism was founded. In the Buddhist tradition, Maya died soon after the birth of Buddha, generally said to be seven days afterward, and came to life again in Hindu-Buddhist heaven, a pattern that is said to be followed in the births of all Buddhas. Thus, Maya did not raise her son in the material world; however, Maya would, on occasion, descend from heaven to advise her son.

In Buddhist literature and art, Queen Maya is portrayed as a beautiful woman in the prime of life.

> *"Her beauty sparkles like a nugget of pure gold. She has perfumed curls like the large black bee. Eyes like lotus petals, teeth like stars in the heavens."*

Gautama forever became the Buddha by attaining the covenant state of spiritual enlightenment when he was 35 years old. He spent the remaining forty-five years of his life sharing insights into human psychology and spiritual practice. While he touched on a wide variety of topics, each of his wisdom-filled lessons was, in some way, intimately connected to the two most important teachings, which serve as the foundational base of Buddhist theology. These are The Four Noble Truths and the Noble Eightfold Path.

The Four Noble Truths

The Buddha conceptualized the Four Noble Truths as:

1. **There is suffering.** (dukkha)
   The truth of suffering is about the desires and cravings of humankind that never seem to be satisfied; desires and pleasure are only temporary, or humans get bored. Unfulfilled, unsatisfied, always chasing the next thing.
2. **There is a cause of suffering.** (samudaya)
   The Buddha's teaching is that the root of all suffering is desire.
3. **There is an end to suffering.** (nirodha)
   The Buddha's teaching is that the way to extinguish desire, which causes suffering, is to liberate oneself from attachments. The end to suffering is the possibility of liberation.
4. **There is a path to end suffering.** (magga)

The eightfold path or the Middle way is the path.

The Noble Eightfold Path

The Noble Eightfold Path[35] is one of the principal teachings of Buddhism; it is designed to help you reach enlightenment. It consists of eight practices, each helping to foster three essential teachings:

1. Ethical Conduct
2. Mental Discipline
3. Wisdom.

The practices are as follows:

1. **Right Understanding** (Samma ditthi)
   See things for how they are and strive to better that which may be unpleasant.
2. **Right Thought** (Samma sankappa)
   Form thoughts of love, compassion, selflessness, and non-violence — in short, think happy thoughts.
3. **Right Speech** (Samma vaca)
   Don't lie, slander, abuse, or ridicule others (even that annoying coworker nobody gets along with).
4. **Right Action** (Samma kammanta)

---

35 https://www.balancedachievement.com/spirituality/noble-eightfold-path/

Conduct yourself peacefully, morally, and honorably.
5. **Right Livelihood** (Samma ajiva)
Don't make a living through corrupt, greedy, or immoral means.
6. **Right Effort** (Samma vayama)
Put in the work necessary to rid your mind of negative and unwanted thoughts.
7. **Right Mindfulness** (Samma sati)
Be conscious of your body, your feelings, your mind, and your ideas.
8. **Right Concentration** (Samma samadhi)
Focus on what is important and stay true to your life's purpose.

It's important to note that all eight disciplines are meant to be practiced at the same time — not one after the other.

20

FINDING CONNECTION IN PARADISE

I am sitting on a tree swing in the beautiful Coco Palm resort in the Maldives island of Duni Kolhu in the Indian Ocean. I arrived here yesterday with my friend Gabi. Gabi is a doctor and lives in Germany. I met her on a desert safari in Dubai, and we connected instantly and became close friends. She suggested that we go to the Maldives for my birthday, so here we are!

Yesterday morning as I was leaving my residence in Dubai, I found a dead pigeon on the ground.

I blessed the bird and sent her soul love and freedom. With this sign, I knew my life was about to change. Whilst seeing a dead bird indicates loss, it's also a sign of difficult times ending and entering new beginnings.

FREE YOUR MIND, LISTEN WITH YOUR HEART

Our flight from Dubai to Male was only four hours long. We then took a small seaplane for 30 minutes to reach our island. When we arrived on the island, it was just me and Gabi. I instantly felt peace and serenity. The weather was warm and calm, the water was turquoise blue and warm, the sand was white and powder-like soft. We can walk around the entire island in about 10 minutes. No cars, no pollution, only the sounds of the birds, the waves, and nature. Also, no need to wear shoes; I have walked barefoot everywhere. I have found my paradise!

I really feel connected to nature here. I feel so peaceful and calm. The stars at night are also incredible. So many stars and so bright. I have never seen such a beautiful sky with so many bright twinkling stars of all sizes. There is magic in every moment here.

This morning, I was awakened by the sounds of the birds, and I went for my morning swim in the warm Indian Ocean. After my swim, Gabi and I walked, barefooted, to the restaurant for our breakfast. When we arrived, we were greeted by a lady by the name of Milan. I said that's an interesting name. I had only heard of it in connection with the city in Italy. "What does it mean?" I asked her. She said, "In my language it means connection." I said it was beautiful and resonated with the feeling I got on this island.

She asked me my name and I told her. She said, "Maya means love in my language." Love and connection meet; it was such a serene moment.

That afternoon after a walk around the island and feeling the connection to nature, I went for a swim in the ocean. I was the only person swimming at that time. I was floating and enjoying the peace and connection to the ocean. In that blissful moment, I started feeling the gentle energy of my mother. I felt like I was a baby again swimming in the womb of my mother before birth. I felt I was being reborn. Tears started rolling down my cheeks; I felt joy, happiness, and love. I felt loved, cared for, and carried by the waters of the ocean and held in the palm of this island.

19th April 2021

Today is Monday, 19th April 2021. It is my 39th birthday. I was also born on a Monday, at 4:40 am, so it's an extra special day for me.

I woke up after having a beautiful dream. My Aunty Zivka (her name means lively or alive in my native language) appeared in my dream. Sadly, she passed away last year after catching the coronavirus. In my dream, she lifted me and gave me a big warm hug. It felt truly amazing. I felt blissful when I woke up to that feeling.

I remember the day she passed away. She came into my dreams that night, too, appearing as a white angel and walking toward me from the heavens. A few hours later, I received a call from my sister with the news that our aunt had passed away that night. I had a feeling that she had ascended because she had appeared as a white angel in my dream and her energy felt very light.

On the morning of my birthday, after breakfast, Gabi and I went snorkeling. We were taken by a small wooden boat to another small island about 20 minutes away, the Robinson Crusoe island. We snorkeled there around the reef. I had not been snorkeling since I was a child; it was lovely to connect with the marine life and the ocean on a deeper level. I saw so many beautiful fish of different shapes and colors, and it was good to see the coral reef in its alive and natural form. It was refreshing to connect to the underwater world. I started thinking about how much unseen life there is under the ocean that most people don't consider. When you see the underwater world, you would think twice before polluting our environment. I was thinking about the connection between the water world and the

FINDING CONNECTION IN PARADISE

land world, and how we are so connected and living in oneness. This truly was a magical experience for me.

On the island, I discovered a turtle rescue and rehabilitation center. They bring turtles that have become hurt in the ocean, mostly by pollution and discarded fishing nets. At the time, there were 10 rescued sea turtles that mostly had only one arm or flipper, where the other had been amputated due to the damage caused when getting caught in old, discarded fishing nets. Some turtles were missing both arms (flippers) and one turtle had heavily damaged organs from the pollution. I became very interested to learn about the turtles and the rescue center. I visited it every day and spent time there with the turtles.

The next day, Gabi and I joined the release of one turtle back into the ocean. Her name was Honu, which means turtle in Hawaiian. Honu had been found entangled in an old fishing net and bucket that some fishermen must have discarded blindly without considering the environment. Honu's front flipper was so badly damaged that it had fallen off and had to be amputated, so she had only one flipper left, and it had taken a couple of months for her to heal and learn to swim and dive again. That day she was ready to go back to her life in the ocean.

I learned that sea turtles are an endangered species. Like humans, they can live up to the age of 100 and become mature at the age of 25. From the thousands of eggs laid, few survive, and this is the reason they are becoming endangered.

I was very happy to discover the sea turtle rescue center, to know that people care and dedicate their time and energy to saving turtles, protecting the environment, and simply appreciating our marine world and what lives within. It truly is a gift to humanity and our planet.

My life lessons and insights during 2020

1. Be humble.
2. Speak less; listen and observe more.
3. Retreat into your own cocoon often.
4. Learn how to love yourself before others can love you.
5. Do what you love and what matters to you; impress yourself, it's not about impressing others.
6. It's what you do behind closed doors and when nobody is watching that really matters. This is who you really are. Let that person come to the light and shine.
7. Be in oneness with nature and animals.

8. Love and be kind; love and kindness are free yet the biggest gifts to humanity.
9. Create a safe and sacred space for yourself to thrive in. Make your home your haven, your sanctuary where you can fully embrace yourself and your creativity.
10. Listening and holding space for others to heal is a real gift.
11. Being is better than doing.
12. Seek balance and harmony in everything you do.
13. Lead by example.
14. Live, love, learn, share.
15. Do everything with love from your heart, openly.

"We think sometimes that poverty is only being hungry, naked and homeless. The poverty of being unwanted, unloved and uncared for is the greatest poverty. We must start in our own homes to remedy this kind of poverty."

— Mother Teresa

www.ingramcontent.com/pod-product-compliance
Lightning Source LLC
Chambersburg PA
CBHW022041160426
43209CB00002B/28